Spur-of-the-Cock

Spur-of-the-Cock

Edited by

J. FRANK DOBIE

SOUTHERN METHODIST UNIVERSITY PRESS : DALLAS

TEXAS FOLKLORE SOCIETY
PUBLICATION NUMBER XI

Facsimile edition 1965

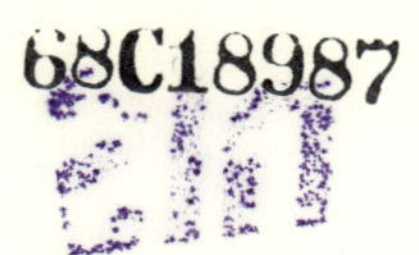

CONTENTS

SPUR-OF-THE-COCK: HERO OF THE MAYO INDIANS*

By HUGH MCGEHEE TAYLOR

INTRODUCTION

In December, 1915, while General Carranza and General Pancho Villa were battling to decide which should save Mexico for the "principles of Madero" and which should "suck the bottle"—as they say in Cuba—and while Mr. Wilson was "watchfully waiting," I was at Mazatlán on the West Coast of Mexico, also waiting. I was waiting to get back to Empalme, near Guaymas, 750 kilometers to the north, as the Sud-Pacifico de Mexico railroad runs.

At San Blas, on the Fuerte River, 320 kilometers to the north, General Emilio Flores commanded a considerable force of *revolucionarios,* well disciplined, with outposts to the north. At Corral on the Yaqui River, 230 kilometers on northward, General Gaxiola commanded about an equal force of poorly disciplined troops with outposts to the south. The Yaqui Indians were on the warpath behind Gaxiola, if not with him. To get to Empalme from Mazatlán I should have to pass through both armies. Of course no trains were running. I had come down the coast without much trouble, but now something had started the *fuerzas,* after months of holding their lines peaceably, to fighting. I knew by experience that if under such conditions I wished to keep the motor car assigned to me by the railroad, I had better not tempt the *valientes* by running it into their midst.

So I left the motor car in Mazatlán and set forth on a lever car with four peons pumping. An old-fashioned hand car like this was too slow and required too much labor to make it a prize for seizure. After an all-day's travel without incident we pumped into San Blas and I at once hunted up General Flores. He was very courteous and told me that I might proceed to my destination, but that, as he did not want any information conveyed to the enemy, he could not allow the operators of the

*Revised by J. Frank Dobie.

lever car to go farther. To pump the car alone was impossible. I went to a little hotel, where room was made for me, and spent the night. The Orient railroad running up from the port of Topolobampo—to stop short against the wall of the Sierra Madre—crosses the Sud-Pacifico at San Blas.

After a night's rest I decided to go down the Orient to the sugar hacienda of Los Mochis and thence to travel overland around the contending armies by an old road, or trail, that follows along the shore of the Gulf of California. The manager at Los Mochis fitted me up with a buckboard, a pair of semi-bronco mules, and a Mayo Indian for a driver. After crossing the Fuerte River with the mules in water and the buckboard on two canoes, we headed for Agiabampo and entered that deserted village just as the sun went down.

Agiabampo used to be something of a port, but the railroads and Topolobampo killed it. From having been a village of two or three thousand people it had dwindled until only five or six families, Mayos, lived there. One of these families said they could find us something to eat—not much, but something. They had no beds or cots but did have *toros*. If a gringo after sleeping—or lying—on such a substitute for a bed all night will rub his body all next day and rub it hard enough, he may rub out the checker-board pattern impressed on him by the mesh of bull-hide thongs that, stretched over a wooden frame, constitute a *toro*.

While the *señora* prepared the supper of turtle (Gulf of California turtle) steak and *tortillas*, the old folk discussed the Revolution; at first they spoke in Spanish but, noting that I listened, they changed to Mayo. Then I tried to make friends with the numerous children of the family. They were sheepish, tongue-tied; they huddled together and just stood off and looked at me. Soon I started telling them one of Uncle Remus's stories, translating freely and liberally. Before I finished, the youngsters were all over me, eyes flashing, breath coming in short gasps. Then at the close, with all the fervor of bull-ring spectators after Mazatini had killed a bull, they called for *otro*. Before I could tell another, however, supper was called. After supper the *señora* started to hustle them off to bed, but they begged *mamacita* to have the *señor* tell just one more story, and the "little mama" relented.

This time the older people listened. The other villagers, who had stolen up to see who and what the visitors were, listened also. They closed in on me like a charmed circle. When I finished, they all demanded *otro.* I told them how Brer Fox became Brer Rabbit's riding horse; I told them about Miss Meadows and the gals. Joel Chandler Harris never had an audience more appreciative. They laughed and yelled, and as Brer Rabbit dashed up to Miss Meadows' house on the back of Brer Fox, jabbing "*cuernavaca*" thorns into his side every time he tried to stop, they rubbed their hands in glee.

They called for another, but this time I pleaded that I was told out and asked them to tell me a story. They admitted that it was their turn and began discussing what should be told and who should tell it. Several stories were suggested. Finally the *señora* of the house suggested that of Totolegoji and nominated Chato (Pugnose), one of the visitors, as the teller. All agreed that this was the story to tell and began discussing how certain terms of Mayo should be rendered in Spanish.

Then Chato stood up and, after thanking me for the unusual stories I had related, said: "The story that follows is one told by the *viejas*—old women—of our tribe. I first heard it when but a *chamusco*[1]—little chap—from my own mother. I have heard it many times since." Again Chato paused to thank me for my stories. Now he launched into the narrative and, standing there in the firelight until it was finished, rarely paused except to ask someone how something should be translated into Spanish. There were some interruptions from his fellow Mayos's suggesting that it was this way or that way. I took notes as best I could and guarded them carefully.

Nearly all the poor people in Mexico stay in their own limited districts and few of them know of anything on the other side of the sierra. The geographical knowledge shown by this unlettered Indian was astounding. He gave name after name of towns, all Indian names, aligning them correctly. I have been

[1] *Chamusco:* an Indian variant or derivative of *chamaco.* I have heard *chamusquito,* the diminutive of a diminutive.

all over the ground. More modern and better known towns of Spanish names are on or near the route traversed by Totolegoji, the hero of the story, but not once did Chato mention them.

As I have already said, I heard this story in 1915. In 1931 I was driving a car alone from San Angelo to Fredericksburg. At a place on the highway I saw a Mexican wanting to ride and picked him up. As soon as I heard him speak and caught sight of his coloring, I knew he was a Mayo. We spoke a few words in Spanish, each looking at the other intently; then we recognized one another as the two story-tellers of Agiabampo. Continued revolutions had driven him to the border, at Nogales. He had worked to El Paso and on east and had been tending sheep in the San Angelo country. His *señora* was dead, he told me, but he had another, for *"el hombre tiene que tener una que hace sus tortillas"*—a man must have someone to make his *tortillas.*

I took Chato to Fredericksburg, fed him, and again came near spending the entire night listening to him talk. He retold the whole story of Totolegoji. I got it all down in Spanish and later read it to him. He approved of the version and said I had it as it was told by the *viejas.* His language was starkly simple; a literal translation was impossible. I have been liberal, at the same time trying to follow the original story exactly.

Many times I have heard Indians of many tribes talking all night; many times I have tried to hear what they were telling. From three different tribes I have gotten a few stories, but in each instance that I got one I was alone with the Indians and won the story by telling first a story to them, by fair exchange, as with Uncle Remus I swapped for Spur-of-the-Cock. This is the kind of swapping that never leaves either swapper the poorer, no matter how valuable the horse he swaps.

The Mayo Indians are indigenous to Sinaloa, belonging linguistically, along with the Yaqui and Tehueco tribes, to the Cahita group. If, as some historians claim—a claim denied by other historians and ethnologists who have a right to opinion,—the Aztecs migrated southward along the West Coast and tarried at Culiacán some eight hundred years ago, they may then have made contact with the Mayos. The origin and significance of the alleged Aztec place names in Sinaloa[2] must be left to scholars. Who beat out the "Gran Camino"—the Great Road—that the hero of the Mayos took on his journey to the Aztec capital will probably never be settled. It was there in pre-Cortez times. As Mr. Carl Sauer has shown in *The Road to Cíbola,*[3] when Coronado proceeded northward to Culiacán, he followed an Indian road "well known and much used"—a road which "the high native culture of Mexico, proceeding ultimately from Mayan Central America, reached as far north as the valley of the Culiacán River on the west coast."

Although the historical Cuitlahuac was brother to Montehcozuma,[4] whom he succeeded, and as leader of the Aztecs routed the Spaniards from the capital, it would seem not unlikely that the tale of the hero Totolegoji, who became Cuitlahuac, originally belonged to an era antedating the conquest.

I. TOTO GROWS UP

Once upon a time a poor woman, half Yaqui and half Mayo, lived in the Valley of Huatebampo, on the Mayo River. She was a widow with one son, a dreamer; and the corn did not grow well at their home for the weeds.

Totolegoji,[5] the boy, or Toto, as his mother called him, would not work but loved to hunt; and young as he was, few men in the tribe could shoot an arrow as quickly or as accurately as could he. From the time he was twelve there was always plenty of meat at their home: venison, birds or wild boar. He and his mother could tan hides beautifully, and they exchanged these with their neighbors for the simple things they required. Flying birds were frequently brought down by him, and rabbits and "jacks" were easy marks whether running or sitting. His mother nearly always had meat to exchange for corn or beans.

---

[2] See *Peregrinación de los Aztecas y Nombres Indígenos de Sinaloa,* por Eustaquio Buelna, Mexico, 1887; revised ed., 1892.

[3] Sauer, Carl, *The Road to Cíbola,* Uni. of Cal. Press, 1932, pp. 1, 6, 33; see also *Azatlán,* by Sauer and Brand, Uni. of Cal. Press, 1932, *passim.*

[4] I have adopted this spelling because it represents the pronunciation as Chato and the Mayo Indians gave it and as various Aztec Indians I have heard give it. The second syllable, which is accented, has always in the mouths of the Indians a *t-e-h* sound.

[5] Totolegoji, a Yaqui word meaning "spur-of-the-cock." Later the hero tires of being called Toto, the Spur, and proclaims himself the Cock.

Toto always listened to any story of adventure anyone had to tell. Tales of encounters with ocelots, panthers, and jaguars and of battles with tribal enemies filled him with fire. He would listen, grab his bow and arrow, and run out in the plains and re-enact the story with himself as the hero, shooting away arrows with little care at trees or mounds of grass. The reeds along the Mayo made fine arrow shanks, and the flints of the foothills made fine points when one knew how to spall them into shape with heat and water.

One evening an uncle of the boy, his father's brother, came to the village. He was a cacique (chief), and was returning from a long trip to the south, where he had called to see the Great Cacique who lived far beyond the sierras. This uncle greatly honored the mother, bringing her syrup, sugar, honey and corn. Toto had brought in a spike-buck just before his kinsman arrived. Now the mother made ready a supper much enjoyed by the cacique and the men with him.

The uncle examined the boy, as tall as himself, his bow, the arrows he had made, and praised him for his good shooting. Then he said to the mother, "In another year if the Yaquis come down from the Bacatetes,[6] you must let Toto come with us to drive them back; he is nearly a man now; it is well enough to kill the meat for you to eat, but to be a man he must meet men in battle."

The mother smiled. "My boy a man?"

After the supper the whole neighborhood came to see and to hear the cacique. He told of his long trip and the wonders he had seen; of tents builded of stones and thatched with grasses; of mountains covered with white powder,[7] of the thousands who lived in the water-surrounded town; of the causeways crossing the lake; of cages of animals, birds and monkeys; of the good food and drink the Great Cacique had provided; of the thousands of men who fought for him anywhere against anyone; of the cacique's wife and her beautiful clothing; of the beau-

---

[6] The Bacatetes ("cow-teats" in vulgar Spanish) are a series of lava-covered mountains, 30 to 80 miles across, lying east of Guaymas, and are still the stronghold of the warlike Yaqui tribe.

[7] Powdered snow. The people who live near sea level south of the Tropic of Cancer have never seen it. I have had several "Costeños" ask me if what they had heard of snow could be the truth.

tiful fat daughter with dimples in her cheeks; and of the excellent dish of *menuda*[8] prepared by her.

"How old is that girl?" asked Toto.

"Why, about fifteen," answered the uncle.

"I am going to marry that girl!" said the boy.

Everyone laughed, the uncle loud and long; and the neighbors, seeing him laugh, all joined in the merriment.

Toto drew himself away. The laughter made him desperate. He went to his bed, lay down, and began to plan.

The uncle soon left with some of the great; then the widow went in and looked at her son; finding him asleep, as she thought, she also lay down to rest.

Toto was up early next morning. He took the hoe and was out in the cornfield long before the sun came up over the sierras. He ran down to the stream and filled everything his mother had that would hold water. Then he was back to the corn and beans. His mother, worried, called him more than once before he would come and eat the breakfast she had prepared for him. He worked hard all day, and when night came the whole field was cleaned of grass and weeds. At supper she had some fat venison broiled for him, but he ate hurriedly and then immediately lay down. He closed his eyes and would say nothing when his mother tried to talk to him. She too closed her eyes, only to worry over her son. Could it be that the laughter and the jibing she and the neighbors had given him had hurt him so?

She lit pine at the fire, brought the burning faggots and looked him over anxiously, put her hand upon his forehead to see if he had fever; but he turned away and pretended that he slept.

II. Toto Prepares to Leave

Early the following morning she heard light footsteps, looked, and saw her son with his bow and a quiver of arrows hurry away across the plain to the foothills. Three hours later he returned bringing in a deer. "Clean this and put the meat in

[8] *Menuda,* tripe hash, is still the dish of dishes with the poor and many of the rich in the "Costa Grande," of Mexico.

the sun," he said. "I killed two"; and he was gone for the second. He was back again before noon, skinned the second deer himself, cut the flesh in strips, and hung them in the sun. Then he stretched the hides, sprinkled them well with salt.

"Now you have meat for a long time," said he. "Watch it and turn it so it will cure well."

"Not so long, Son," she answered. "You eat a great deal now."

"But I will not be here for a long time," he said. "I go to marry the Great Cacique's daughter."

"Son," she said, "don't think any more of that. If you want a wife, look at Nepo's daughter. She is strong, fat, a good cook; is always laughing and could be the mother of many sons. Look in her eyes when she talks to you. You are no cacique, not even a man yet; the Great Cacique would probably chain you with the monkeys if you asked for his daughter."

"But I am going to leave tomorrow, and I am going to marry her before I return!"

The mother said nothing. She knew men and that there was no use in further words. She wrapped the bed skins about her and lay down but did not sleep.

The next morning Toto was up early, his *maleta* (a bag) filled with the few things he had; he took all the arrow points he had made, his bow, his quiver. He came, and looked at his mother, who sprang up, caught him by the shoulder, and turned his face to hers.

His jaw was set, determination was in his eyes. "Well," said she, "if you will go, go by the cavern where the Oracle lives. Tell him what you wish to do and do what he says, even to coming home and never thinking of that girl again."

Toto promised to abide by the Oracle's instructions, gently removed his mother's hands, bounded away, and went toward the sierras—toward the great hole through which the sun rolls back east at night to rise and come above in the mornings. There where the water comes dashing down is a great cavern on the right, and in this the Great Oracle lives.

The time was the early *primavera* (the spring). An early rain had brought out the flowers: the yellow fragrant *huisache,* the faint, sweet *quebrantilla,* heliotrope-like in odor, and the purple *palo hierro* already dropping its lovely purple bells in the streams.

Toto was moving with the rapid, smooth fox trot of the Indian; his feet barely lifted from the ground. On and on, he trotted up the valley. He had had nothing to eat in the morning and toward noon he felt hunger; he slowed down and turned south into a valley full of prickly pear. Before he saw the covey of top-knotted quail his arrow was drawn; his bow twanged and one fell over. The other birds flushed, but he watched their flight and lighting, and stalked them rapidly; soon he brought down a second bird. Then taking them to the stream, he cleaned them. Now he took out two pieces of tinder, rubbed them into fire, and roasted the birds.

After his meal, on he went again. The plains had given way now to rolling hills, paralleling the sierras, each hill higher than the one last passed. Suddenly, just at sunset, he reached the foot of the sierras. Around a bend in the stream he saw a deer and fawn drinking. The fawn fell with an arrow through its heart. In a few moments the flesh was roasting on a fire.

Then Toto found a niche on a boulder, high up on the stream's side, difficult to reach. There he slept, with hooting owls waking him now and then. On the morrow he roasted the rest of the fawn, ate that, and went on till he came to the cavern of the Oracle.

III. THE ORACLE:[9] WHAT HE SAID

At the entrance Toto paused long enough for his eyes to become accustomed to the half light. Then he went on till he came to a stout door closed. He opened this without knocking. He entered a great chamber and faced a long glassy-fingered rock pointing down and pointing up. Light from somewhere above was reflected here and there, making great shadows. There was no furniture anywhere, but straight ahead there was a large coffin-like box on end. In front of the box was a small

[9] Bernal Diaz and Gertrudis Gomez de Avellameda both tell of Montehcozuma's consultation of oracles, proving that they were not unknown in ancient Mexico.

opening, something like the opening over the shelf of a *padre's* confession box. Toto walked over to this. At the sound of a great voice his blood ran cold.

"*Quién es?* (Who is it?) Ah, Totolegoji, what do you here?"

"*Señor,*" said the boy, "you know who I am. I wish to go to the home of the Great Cacique, to wed his daughter, to be a great warrior. Shall I go, or shall I stay?"

"Not so fast," said the Oracle.

"He who would great things have done
Must not attempt them all alone!
Counsel to follow you will do well,
For it has cost you one *real.*"

The great voice was silent then, but a long skinny arm came around the corners of the box, the hand, palm up, held for the money.

Toto looked in his *maleta,* found a decimo and two coppers,[10] and dropped them in the open palm. The hand was pulled back behind the coffin, and the voice came again:

"Never part from the King's Highway,
However beauteous or short the byway.
Counsel to follow you'll do well,
But this counsel costs you one *real.*"

The long arm came around the corners again with the upturned palm; the boy again counted into it a dime and two coppers. "Is there anything else?" asked the boy.

"He who would please the fair
Must be careful what to wear.
Counsel to follow you'll do well,
For this counsel costs you one *real.*"

The arm and palm came back, and the boy again counted out the money.

[10] The *real* (bit) of two cents and a dime is quite modern. The old Spanish *real* was 12½ *centavos.*

"Is there anything else? Will I marry the girl?"

"Fear naught in heaven, nor from the earth,
Nor yet the yellow beast in hell.
Counsel to follow you'll do well,
For it has cost you one *real*."

Toto counted the money again into the palm, the hand was withdrawn, and then all was silent.

He, boylike, begged to know whether, if he did all the Oracle had counselled, he would get the girl. But the Oracle answered nothing at all.

Toto waited some little time. He was on his knees through no sense of devotion, but because his knees trembled and he could not stand. After a while the thought came to him that the Oracle had not bid him return home as his mother wished. He arose, picked up his bow and arrows, bowed low, and left.

IV. "MUST BE CAREFUL WHAT TO WEAR"

As Toto emerged from the cavern into daylight, delight came to him. He started on a run down to the plains, his sandals clattering on the stones till long after noon.

In a forest of large trees he halted. Hunger had begun to pull at his entrails, and he began to hunt. A queer nest hanging from an epiphyte met his eyes between the swaying wisps of long gray moss. A glitter of green and blue, a crested head shone from one side of the suspended nest; this and the long tail hanging out the other side told him that the bird was a quetzal,[11] the male on the nest while the female hunted food.

"He who would appear before the fair must be careful what to wear," Toto thought. His bow twanged and he picked up the bird.

"A fine headdress indeed!" and he carefully removed the skin with all the feathers. He ate the bird, washed the bird's skin carefully, preening the feathers, fashioned a fibre band to fit his head, and bound the skin over it. Later he found some *quebracho* [*quiebra-hacha*, break-axe, a hardwood] trees and

[11] The *quetzal*, associated with the worship of Quetzalcoahuatl, the Plumed Serpent, was worshiped either as a deity or as the symbol of a deity, by both the Mayans and Aztecs.

removed the bark, taking as much as he needed for the tannin. He had nothing to steep the bark in, but later in the day he found some *guajes* (gourds) growing on trees. He split several of these to make vessels for holding the bark in solution.

He travelled on till dark. He had shot a "jack" for supper and eaten it. He kept going till he reached the beach. He felt down this till he found the salt water, filled his gourds, and ground up the bark and put it to soak. An hour later he was sprinkling the bird skin with the mixture, inside and out, handling it carefully to save the feathers. Then he hung the skin high on a bush, rolled up some sedge grasses, and went to sleep.

He was up early on the morrow, awakened by the snort and the rapid hoof-beats of a startled buck running toward him. An arrow was quickly fitted to the bow, and the buck dropped dead a few yards beyond him. He fitted another arrow with a sharp point and lay watching for what had frightened the buck. There was a movement in the sedge; then in the faint dawn he caught from the grass the icy gleam of a greenish pair of eyes under black and tawny markings. A second later the jaguar, the thing that had been following the buck, winded him, and with a blood-curdling scream charged. Toto waited till the animal was within ten paces, and took him on the rise. The arrow entered under the throat and pierced the heart. The beast fell almost at his feet.

Then Toto laughed; he held his head high, his chin drawn in closely to his throat. He had slain the king of all the bosques and was a man!

He got out his tinder and made a fire, ran quickly and skinned the buck, cooked meat, and ate his breakfast. Then he put all his bark to steep. Now he skinned the large beast, nearly as long again as he was high. He got large flat stones and laid them down; then with salt and sand and a small stone he rubbed the skin clean of all fats. Next he stretched the hide and sprinkled it liberally with tannin. He went back to the *quebrachos* and got more bark and put it to steep. Late in the afternoon he worked the skin again until it was pliant; he again added salt and a liberal supply of tannin.

"He who would appear before the fair must be careful what

to wear," kept running through his head. The quetzal skin received another dressing. He folded the jaguar skin and slept that night with it beneath his head. The third day he repeated the curing process with both skins. The quetzal, now pliant and soft, fitted his head nicely. The fourth day, under almost constant rubbing in and out of the tannin, the jaguar skin became pliant to the feel.

The fifth day Toto dressed in his new apparel. With the plumes on his head and the spotted jaguar skin draped around him, he went down to a quiet pool of clear water and there at himself gazed for a long, long time. He was well satisfied. "I am now Legoji," he said. "No longer may anyone call me Toto." Then again he took the trail south, the personification of haughty dignity.

In the afternoon he came to Cajeme, where there were members of his tribe known to him. He called on them but was too haughty, and left them soon, on his way south. The following day he reached and crossed the Fuerte River, leaving his kin behind.

V. THE GIANTS[12] ROMPERÓN AND SOPLÓN

Just as he reached the tableland, he spied a giant in the trail ahead. In his hands the giant carried two enormous stones that he was grinding to powder. When one stone was ground away, he picked up another and ground that also. He was half as tall again as Legoji and would weigh as much as four of him.

"What are you doing, my friend?" asked Legoji.

The giant turned and, stretching out his great arms, answered, "Just grinding stones, son. Come here till I grind your bones to powder."

Legoji advanced. "Fear naught on earth, nor in heaven or hell!" he thought, and smiled.

---

[12] "The notion that the ancient habitants of these lands were giants is so common among all the authors who have written on affairs of the Indies that hardly one will be found who does not refer to them," says D. Mariano Veytia, in *Historia Antigua de Mejico*, Mexico, 1836, I, 144; and the same author, pp. 143–153, speaks of fossil remains verifying "living traditions" of giants among the indigenes. He quotes in particular Torquemada (q. v., ed. 1723, I, 36–38) and Clavigero (q. v., ed. 1844, Bk. II, 51).

Where did the Llano de los Gigantes, in western Coahuila and eastern Chihuahua, get its name?

"These little arrows will quiet you to carrion for the vulture awaiting there!" he said, pointing beyond him. As the giant turned to look, *twang* sounded the bow, and an arrow pierced his right ear. The giant whirled with a roar and another arrow pierced the left ear. So quickly it was hardly seen, a third arrow was on the bow, the string pulled taut. "It will be your heart this time," said Legoji. "Stop!"

The giant had never before seen anyone so quick. He stopped, pulled the shafts out of his ears, and advanced, holding them out to Legoji.

"Who are you?" demanded the giant.

"The cacique Legoji." True, he was a prince by blood and now by bravery also. "Who are you?" he asked.

"I'm the rompedor Romperón,[13]
The strongest giant ever born,"

he said.

"Ah!" thought Legoji, "He who would great things have done must not attempt them all alone. I must have that man with me." Then he added aloud, "What are you doing here, Romperón?"

"Nothing; I have no home, have nothing to eat. I am alone, hungry, too, sir."

"Well, come with me," said Legoji. You shall have plenty of food; I have need of your great strength."

He walked ahead without looking back and Romperón followed. Soon Legoji saw a deer, and, shedding his finery, which he told Romperón to bring, he bounded away faster than the deer itself. He fitted an arrow to his bow as he ran, and as the deer turned a bit to avoid a tree, dropped her dead with an arrow. Romperón had never seen a man so fleet. He came running up, all out of breath, but helped skin the doe and cut the meat in strips. He gathered wood while Legoji kindled a fire. They were soon eating. The giant ate long and never ceased admiring Legoji.

"You are a cacique, a great hunter, too. With reason you wear the great cat's skin."

---

[13] *Romper,* to break; *rompedor,* the breaker; *Romperón,* the giant, or great, breaker.

This was very sweet to Legoji. He listened with grave pride, smiling a very little lest he appear too easily pleased. He gave the skin to Romperón as he had nothing, showed him how to tan the skin, then to fold it up with the remaining meat inside. They went on south.

Approaching the Río Guamúchil, they were astonished to see a cloud of dust not far beyond. The wind blew a sudden gale, nearly upsetting Romperón and sending Legoji racing after his headgear blown entirely away. After the wind came the sound as of a great cough, but there was no cloud and no thunder.

"What in the world caused that gale?" Legoji said to the giant.

"Look! Yonder! There is a giant as great as myself!"

True enough, this new giant had an enormous mouth, throat, and lungs; his breast was shaped much like a bellows; his legs were small for a creature so large.

He had seen them and was calling: "Come on, Little Men. I beg pardon; I thought no one was near and opened my mouth too wide."

"Little Men?" roared Romperón. "I am as large as you. Turn your head the other way when you cough. Your breath smells foul."

"Why, who are you?" demanded he. "I will blow you out to sea!"

"And who are you?" yelled Romperón. "I will grind your bones to powder!" At the same time, picking up two enormous stones, he crushed them in his hands. Both giants walked forward till only the little stream lay between them.

"He who would great things have done, must not attempt them all alone," thought Legoji. "I must have that other giant also."

"But that you may know you would never touch my bones, my brother, watch that tree," the strange giant said.

He took a deep breath, turned to the tree, opened his mouth, gave a great cough. The tree—trunk, roots and branches—was gone. Then he turned back to the "Little Men" laughing. He was a good-humored giant, as most giants are.

Romperón was sullen, but he admired the other and said: "Well, who are you, brother?"

"I'm the sopla fuelle, Soplón,[14]
The greatest blowhard ever born!"

Then he laughed again. A gull that was passing lost all its feathers and fell into the water squawking.

"Say, brother, lie down on your back and look straight up if you are going to laugh any more," said Romperón, laughing also. Then he stepped across the water, and they shook hands.

Soplón was hungry and asked if they had anything to eat. Legoji kindled a fire and they were soon feasting. Legoji could eat little; Romperón always seemed to be able to eat yet more. They soon finished the doe meat. Then Soplón asked where they were going. Legoji answered, "South along the great trail, to the home of the Great Cacique."

"Might I go with you also?" asked Soplón.

With marked condescension, Legoji gave him permission, but he asked, "Your legs, can they lift you up the great sierras?"

"I was born in the sierras," answered the giant. "A little food regularly, a little patience, and my legs can carry me anywhere. If not, I know how to get up the sierras in a manner easier than any you know."

"All right," said Legoji. "Come on. Your raiment needs renewal, but there are animals and they have skins."

He started ahead, Romperón behind him, and Soplón following. A deer soon fell to Legoji's arrow. The giants skinned it. Legoji kindled the fire, and they were eating again. Soplón was given this skin. They went on till night, taking half the deer with them.

Soplón asked for some of the cracklings, which he ate. He rubbed the suet into his legs. He knew that to be fleet one must eat animals of great pace, and that rubbing in the fat of the deer would make his legs supple and strong.

---

[14] *Sopla fuelle* means literally one who blows the bellows, bellows-blower. *Soplón*, the great blower, if not very good Spanish, is a good word.

VI. THE BANDITS OF THE BYWAY

They started early next morning and made excellent time. Legoji seemed never to tire; Romperón was now hardened and could keep up. Soplón after several hours began to tire on his thin legs and fell behind. Legoji shot another deer. The two giants ate all that Legoji did not require. The suet was again worked into Soplón's legs; the force of the deer rubbed in became a part of him. His endurance soon equaled that of Romperón, but neither could endure like Legoji. He had eaten deer nearly all his life.

Crossing the Sierra de Tepic, they overtook a wedding party full of food and laughter. These asked where the cacique and his powerful followers were bound.

"To see the Great Cacique in the south."

One of the young men, an amiable fellow, told them of a short path over the sierras which would save them a day as against the more circuitous highway. Romperón and Soplón both said at once, "Let's take the *vereda* (trail)."

But the Oracle's words came to Legoji:

> "Never part from the King's highway,
> However beauteous or short the byway."

"No," he said, "we go the highway."

They proceeded and that night found how well they had done. The same young man came into camp, falling exhausted as he reached them; he told how his party had proceeded but a short distance after their separation from Legoji when they were set upon by a well armed band of thieves. "And I am the only one left alive to tell the tale," he concluded.

Legoji was indignant. He counted his arrows. Romperón began picking up and placing in his *maleta* smooth round stones. Soplón took up nothing, but the good-humored giant was so angry that his breathing lifted his shoulders up and down.

"Lead us back there. We will punish those *bandidos,*" said Legoji.

First, though, the three eager ones fed the exhausted youth with deer meat. His name was Naulach. When he had had his fill, his limbs became as agile and his eyes as sharp as those of a stag. He led them back and they reached the bandit camp just at dawn. The bandits had made a night of it. A warrior was recounting his escapades and boasting of other expected encounters. "We fear not the cacique of Michoacán, nor the Great Cacique of the south," he shouted amid much applause. "Let them send their warriors after us; we will lead them into the defiles of the sierras and not a man of them will live to take home the story of their defeat."

Legoji fitted an arrow to his bow and from a distance of three hundred paces let drive at the orator. It pierced his body just under the left arm and he fell forward dead.

All eyes had been upon him; in speaking he had been turning this way and that; so none could tell whence the arrow came. The *bandidos* ran together to see what had happened to their leader.

"You get under that crag yonder," Legoji said to the youth Naulach. "Soplón, you go with him. Romperón, you stay with me. When you hear the *macaca* call, let drive!" A low cat's call told Legoji when his men had made the crag. At once he made the cry of the great macaw parrot. A priest and a cacique dropped from two arrows. The *bandidos* ran together again, but before Legoji could call a second time he heard at his side, *U-m-m-m-ph!*

Romperón had tossed a great handful of stones into the crowd. Many fell never to rise again. The direction from which the stones came was easily told. Those not wounded charged up the slope, to meet another handful of the stones. Many fell again, but the charge kept on, the *bandidos* scattering as they came. Legoji and the youth shot as fast as they could fit arrows to their bows, Romperón tossed again and again, but on the enemy came. As they reached the rise running back to the crag, a great cough was heard. Trees, rock, and men went down; the great *fuelle* Soplón had begun to fight. This was new warfare to the thieves. "Huitzil!" came the cry as one saw Romperón. The men stopped, whirled about, and all who could run ran as they never ran before in their lives, leaving their dead, wounded, and plunder behind.

Legoji and his retainers went down to the fire, Romperón dropping a stone on any who moved or moaned. Some of the thieves looked back, saw the silhouette of the giants, saw Legoji's waving plumes, and, believing the God of Winds, the God of War, and the Fair God were back on earth, lost no time in putting all distance possible behind them.

Legoji took the string of turquoise worn by the leader he had first downed. The giants parted the balance of the plunder, giving to Naulach what he would take; he too was given a fine neck piece. Both he and Legoji had all the arrows their quivers would hold.

The four continued their journey south, and days later crossed Lake Chapala at its lower end, circled the lake and came to near Tínguindín. Before reaching the town, they saw a warrior running to them like a deer.

"Thousands of dwarf Guajes[15] are besieging the town!" he called.

Legoji and his followers had never heard of the dwarfs. The warrior explained that they had been besieging the town for days. Food was running low. He had charged out at orders of his cacique, and had gotten through by a miracle. He was to call the cacique of Michoacán but feared that however quickly help might come it would come too late.

VII. The Battle of the Dwarfs

Legoji and his men consulted, then planned the battle. Soplón was sent with the escaped warrior to the south to the gap leading to Lake Zacapu, where the road crossed the divide over an ash heap from the old Volcano of Inky Waters. On the divide Soplón was to raise a great cloud of dust as of many warriors running, then come on down the slope raising another, and yet another. Legoji with Naulach and Romperón would go to the north to the narrow defile leading to Guanajuato. Legoji would wait until he was sure Soplón had reached the divide; then he would shoot a fiery arrow high in the sky as a signal for Soplón to raise the dust.

Romperón filled his *maleta* with rounded flints as he walked.

[15] Oviedo's *Historia de las Indias*, as quoted by Prescott, speaks of the "dwarfs and buffoons" that Montehcozuma had in his dining hall. Small Indians known as Guajes still live in Santa Cruz, between Celaya and Guanajuato.

They got in place and when sufficient time had elapsed, Legoji wrapped dried grasses around an arrow, fired the grasses, and shot it high. Almost at once a cloud of dust arose in the gap; this grew and was lifted along the route down to the pines growing on the slope.

There was a hush in the cries of besiegers and besieged. Then came the cry, "Los Tarascos!"

The Guajes broke pellmell for the pass to the north above which Legoji and his men were hidden. As the leaders came nearly opposite him, Legoji said to Romperón, "Give them some eggs!"

The giant tossed the handful, and quickly filled his right hand from his left and tossed again. His first volley took the leaders; many fell and more than were wounded fell over the fallen. There was great disorder. When the second handful reached the dwarfs, the disorder was complete.

A little warrior running to the right, a guard covering the flank, came tearing through the brush. He saw the giant with the youths gathering and handing him stones. He raised the cry of "Huitzil!" Lifting the point of his spear, he charged directly at what he supposed to be a god. Legoji's arrow stopped his cry and stopped short his life, but others saw the giant and they too cried, "Huitzil!"

Running ahead, as they came out of the pass they scattered as do quail when a *tecolotl* (hawk) swoops down on them, right, left and center. Two of the rear guard came through the brush, bodies so close to the ground as they ran that they were very near before they were seen. Legoji's arrow again accounted for the first; Naulach hit the second; but the little warrior ran on a short distance and just as he fell tossed his spear at Romperón. The great fellow dropped flat, but had not Naulach thrown himself in the path of the spear it would have pierced the giant's body. One of Legoji's followers was dead.

With a second arrow Legoji caught the wounded Guaje in the stomach, and he sang the sleeping song. Just then the besieged warriors began to arrive, not having waited for the expected aid. They ran after the flying dwarfs, killing them where overtaken, or were themselves killed. So many of the Guajes had been killed or wounded that they were now outnumbered. But they fought every foe overtaking them. Many escaped to their homes with tales of Huitzil's return to earth and of his helping their enemies the Tarascos. The Guajes moved back into their hills to hide.

VIII. RECEIVED AS GODS BY THE TARASCOS

Certain Tarascos who saw the youth take the spear intended for Romperón and then Legoji shoot the dwarf, stopped. They saw the giant lift the youth in his arms and feel for his heart. It was still; tears filled his eyes. The Tarascos cried, "Huitzil! Huitzilopochtli!"[16]

"I am but a giant and this is my cacique," said Romperón, indicating Legoji. He put down the youth, stood a moment with folded arms, and then, pointing down in the pass to the dead and wounded Guajes, said, "That is what we did!"

Just then Soplón came running up, dropped on his knees, felt the pulse of the dead boy, and tears filled his eyes.

"Do not weep," said Legoji. "He gave his life to save that of a friend and to retrieve his own poor shooting. He was a brave man."

The messenger came up, explained to the Tarascos the ruse by Soplón at Legoji's orders, and that no one was coming from Pátzcuaro.

"Then we were saved by you, my cacique, you and your strange men," said Parapeo, the local chief. "One of yours lost his life. Come with me and we will show you how we care for our friends."

This cacique was short, black-brown in the manner of the Tarascos. His hair was greying, as was the moustache of a

[16] Huitzilopochtli, god of war among the Aztecs. The only gods mentioned by Chato and his fellow Mayos were Huitzilopochtli and Quetzalcoahuatl. The "God of Winds" was so called in the Spanish spoken to me; I asked for his name and also for the names of the other gods in Mayo. The Mayos replied that they had no such gods and therefore had no names for them.

few straight hairs.[17] He looked over and wondered at Soplón and Romperón, but his eyes filled with admiration at the sleek yellow-brown skin of Legoji. He took Legoji by the arm, pushed him ahead, and followed the young chief to the village.

The best food they had was set before the visitors, with the sour sweet pulque—the first Legoji had ever drunk. Maidens were called, and they were present at once. Mothers and wives followed; messengers ran over the divide for fresh fish and hunters were sent for game. Then the old cacique drew himself up beside Legoji where all could see them and told what this great friend had done. Then he invited Legoji to take his pick of all the maidens, to remain with her and them.

Legoji thanked him, but said, "Among so many beautiful women how could one ever make choice?"

The strangers were weary from the long tramp. The cacique soon saw this, and turned over to them his *cuarto para distinguidos* (room for the distinguished). They did not sleep well that night. Warriors were constantly returning, some bringing dead friends killed by the dwarfs' sharp spears. Others came wounded; their wounds had to be dressed. Many came delighted and had to recount their exploits. There was too much noise to permit sleep for men who had spent so many nights with no sound at all except the stealthy movements of the one on guard, as he replenished the fires to keep off the animals, the spirits, and *brujas* (witches), all of which fear the fire.

The next morning early food was ready at the cacique's home. Legoji, as soon as this was eaten, gravely thanked the chief and those serving him and said, "I must be on my way!"

He would have left, but the cacique said, "I am an old man. I know so distinguished a man has some business. My home is your home. Come when you will. If you go to Quiroga,

[17] Judging from terra cotta heads dug up in San Pedro between Oaxaca and Tavichi, from heads represented in the walls of Mitla, and from other representations that have come down there must have been a bearded race in Mexico. In a village called Ixtlahuaca—not the village of that name in the tale—southwest of Toluca, near the state line of Mexico and Guerrero, live a tribe of Indians the men of which have an unusual amount of beard and all the members of which have grey-blue eyes unlike any eyes I have seen elsewhere in Europe or America. These people spoke neither Spanish, Aztec, nor Tarascan, and we were unable to communicate with them.

Pátzcuaro, Apatzingán, or Maravatio, I have friends and relatives at all these places and will gladly send a fleet runner to let them know you are a friend to all Tarascos. It will make your way easy."

Legoji thanked him, told him he would pass through Quiroga, but that it would take him a day longer to go through Pátzcuaro, as to go that way he would have to walk around the lake.

"But," replied the old chief, "I have canoes and paddlemen who are at the landing. I will send them orders to cross you and your men in my canoes, to treat you with the same care and deference as if I myself were traveling. I will send advice to our cacique, the lord of all the Tarascos. He will take delight in courtesy to the cacique of the Mayos."

Legoji could but accept; either route around the lake meant at least an extra day, and the more eastern route was over difficult lands, although a day shorter. He found the lake a thing of beauty. Tree clad spurs from the sierras ran down into the fresh green-blue water; thousands of water-birds, some of which he had never seen, were on its surface.

A runner had crossed the lake ahead of Legoji. When Legoji and his giants landed on the south shore, the cacique of Michoacán was there to receive him as an equal and a friend.

Campos was the head chief of the Tarascos, his subjects but slightly inferior in number to the Mejicanos themselves. His capital was Quiroga, his summer home at Pátzcuaro, his winter home at Apatzingán, on the Río Balsas.

Campos's empire reached the waters of the setting sun; Montehcozuma's, the waters of the rising sun. Campos was a great friend of the Nahuatl emperor, and their warriors frequently fought together against others who stood in their way or disputed their control. Neither of the chiefs fought any longer now; their sons or chieftains selected by them fought in their stead, the old ones remaining at home.

When they were younger, they had fought each other at Huamuxtitlán, where all the fighters on both sides were slain. Only the two chiefs remained alive, and they fought till both were exhausted, until neither could fit an arrow to a bow, toss a spear, or lift the obsidian-studded club. Both were wounded, and both fell at the same time. Campos recovered first and was about to slay his enemy when Montehcozuma said, "Water!"

Campos could not slay him; he brought the water, bathed the Aztec's wounds and his own, found medicinal herbs and dressed their wounds. Montehcozuma revived, and thanked the dark friend who had been his enemy.

When they were fully recovered, they went to a sierra. There the Aztec said, "Here is the line between us; from Citlaltepec (the Nevada de Toluca) to Tetepac El Viejo and on to the blue sea in the west is the line. You will not come south. I will not go north. From Citlaltepec to Amealco and on toward Polaris is the other line. You will not go over it toward the rising sun; I will not cross it toward the setting sun. Do you agree?"

Campos laughed, then sighed, "My brother, had we talked first we would not have fought and all those lying dead yonder would have been alive. We will not fight more."

Now Campos was old and the priests had much to say. When they saw the giants, they whispered one to another, "The God of War and The God of Winds are with that youth. If he were white and had a long beard, we would know he was Quetzalcoahuatl; perhaps he has changed himself as have these others, eating and drinking like men. Treat them fairly; they go to Montehcozuma, perhaps for no good."

Campos said, "My brother of Tínguindín has sent me word that those giants and the young cacique they serve have killed hundreds of the hornet dwarfs, the Guajes. They who have saved my brother and his people cannot be my enemies."

The priests did not believe the giants were men. The men who had accompanied Legoji from Tínguindín told of how the ruse had been worked and how Romperón had rained down thousands of round rocks and how hundreds, even thousands, of the hornets were killed. Each time they told the story, the number of the slain was added to. Hoping ruin for the Aztecs, whom they detested, the priests counseled Campos to treat them with distinction and to hurry them on to Montehcozuma.

The priests of the Mexicans hated the Tarascos as much as they were hated. Outbreaks between the two nations were frequent; but the unquestioned friendship between the two chieftains kept all but small outbreaks under control. Into all questions between their followers each looked with care. Many Aztecs had their hearts torn out on the pyramid of Huitzil; Campos's favorite punishment for his men when they were in the wrong was to tie stones to their feet and toss them into Pátzcuaro lake to feed the fishes.

Campos treated Legoji with the greatest distinction; the young cacique's people, the Mayos, lived too far north for him to have any knowledge of them. He had been told there was such a people, but those telling of them had as little knowledge as he. Time and again he tried to worm out of Legoji his purpose for journeying south; but the young man would smile, thinking of the princess whose name he did not know, and keep his own counsel. Legoji was shrewd enough to keep Romperón and Soplón away from the priests and from Campos. They spoke a tongue Legoji himself was but beginning to learn; they also spoke Mayo and Aztec, but neither spoke Tarascan.

Legoji thought best to show the Tarascos one day just what his followers could do. He took them beyond Lake Charahuen and had Romperón grind up rocks and Soplón scatter the fragments with a breath over the country toward Tancítaro. The malpais is still there. Campos was impressed by what he saw and wished the giants and Legoji a happy ending of their long trip.

He dispatched a rapid courier to the Aztec, told him he believed the strangers were gods, and that they were coming to visit him as Quetzalcoahuatl had visited his ancestors. If the Aztecs showed wisdom in his treatment of them, he advised, all would be well. He promised to keep the Great Cacique advised of their progress forward. The first messenger got to Mexico, but the second was overtaken by the strangers. This runner returned, notifying Campos that they had passed him at Tultenango. It was impossible, he said, to outrun gods. Tultenango was outside the domain of Campos; he heaved a sigh of relief but feared for his friend.

IX. MONTEHCOZUMA'S WARRIORS BLOWN DOWN

There were deer, not so many, but thousands of doves eating the seed of the cosmos, purple, brick dust, and white colored. Legoji shot these as he ran along, and now and then he killed a deer. They did not hunger.

They passed up the valley of the Lerma to Ixtlahuaca, and from there struck a bee line over the sierras to Azcapotzalco. As they reached the summit just after daylight one morning, the snow-crowned Ixtaccihuatl, with snow well down on her sides, came into view. Beyond her was Popocatepetl, the snow reaching across the saddle between them. Legoji and the giants stopped in wonder at the beauty of the sight. Texcoco Lake lay in the flat below them, occupying more than half of it. Legoji felt humble at the beauty, as many others have felt.

They were interrupted by sight of an army on march coming toward them. The same kind of malpais over which Legoji had run since a child was close on his left—lava beds in broken loose cubes from the size of a fist to the size of a house. His Yaqui training had taught Legoji to race over this at full speed. Romperón and Soplón could not get over it at all. Into a large pit to one side he hurried the giants. But he saw they had been seen, and he told his henchmen to get ready for trouble.

He stood in the open and when the strange soldiers were close enough to be seen distinctly, he lifted his right hand straight above his head and watched for an answer. The army was halted. Apparently there was some discussion among the leaders. Then the chieftain, lifting his hand in like position, walked forward.

When a few paces off, the chieftain halted, saluted, and asked, "Who are you and what do you here without the Great Cacique's permission?"

Legoji was easily a half head taller than the other but not nearly so stout. He said, "I am the cacique of the Mayos of Navahoa."

"The Mayos we know not. The Mayas we know well. They live in the south and not in the north. Where is the land, and what the number and size of the people?"

Legoji answered, "Size? I am a Mayo. Look at me. We

live on the western great waters; in number we are many *tzontles, tzontles.* [A *tzontle* is 400.] Who are you, my brave friend?"

"I am the head of the army here, in Montehcozuma's service. I am Aztec. Who are those great beings I saw with you but a moment since?"

"Those are friends of mine. Why do you ask?"

"It's my business to ask. You will do well to answer quietly and truthfully, or you will never see the Great Cacique, and never get home!"

"Do you think your little army frightens me?" said Legoji. "I have seen armies before. You are no doubt brave, but I must ask you to stand aside and allow me and my two men to pass. Otherwise, take the consequences."

"Take the consequences?" mocked the other. "What can you do?" He lifted an obsidian-studded war club and advanced threateningly.

Quick as a flash Legoji fitted an arrow to his bow and shot him through the biceps of his right arm. He caught the club with the left hand and kept on coming. A second arrow tore through the biceps of the left. The arm dropped to his side, useless as was the other. The Aztecs rushed forward, but Legoji ran to one side. "Upset them, Soplón!" he called.

The giant stepped forward and, as Legoji reached safety, coughed and coughed again.

Montehcozuma's army, picked men, were routed—blown over one another and rolled down to the foot of the slope.

Legoji stepped forward, picked up his antagonist, who had been blown a hundred paces, set him on his feet, pulled the shafts of the arrows from his arms, and told him he could go.

"Go?" said the other. "Back to Montehcozuma? You do not know him. I was sent to stop you, slay you if need be. I am useless now as a warrior. I can fight no more. My army is gone, blown to pieces by that god there. Back to Montehcozuma? Take the war club there and end it all."

Legoji picked up the club, swung it, and with one blow gave him sleep.

Then he looked over the wounded smashed against stones, called the two giants, and had them search till they found two who from their dress and pride were evidently sub-chieftains, and not greatly hurt. Then they bathed the wounds and gave the two a little food.

Legoji said, "Go back to your master, tell him what you have seen. Tell him that I come as a friend to seek the Great Cacique's favor. I have somewhat to ask of him and regret I had to punish his discourteous servants. We will follow you to his home. Tell those en route I do not wish to slay but to be friends with the Mexicanos! But if there be any treachery, beware! We will know! Get you gone!"

The two men ran as they had never run before. Others running were overtaken and learned what Legoji had said. "Their officers were killed. Should they stop and fight? Fight gods? No!"

Legoji followed, stopped for the night at the village of the Otomies, who hated the Aztecs bitterly. He was royally received by them.

Early the next morning they were on their way again and before night reached Azcapotzalco, where all houses were closed and no one was in sight.

With considerable trouble they found an inn, and asked for food and lodging. The host, when he saw the giants, dropped to his knees, begging them to go farther; he had a very humble house, unworthy of such great caciques.

Legoji laughed. "An humble home is honored by great guests, my man. Up, prepare us a meal for five men."

The meal was prepared and eaten in silence, Legoji wondering how he could reach the city if Montehcozuma did not invite him to cross the carefully guarded causeways.

X. RECEIVED BY MONTEHCOZUMA

The old Coyote, however, sent peaceful messengers, who reported to Legoji almost at once after his arrival at the inn. These were priests and great men, near the Great Cacique himself. Legoji received them with distinguished gravity. They asked many questions, but the only answer given was that Legoji had come as a suitor for the princess; that he wished to see the Great Cacique.

He in turn asked many questions about their religion, about the extent of the empire, about the Mayas, and seemed to them to know their answers before they had spoken. They apologized for the affronts of the defeated warrior and told Legoji Montehcozuma had deprived the man's family of all the honors he had won. This warrior had also been a candidate for the princess's hand, and no doubt that had made him rude.

"Tell the princess I regret depriving her of a suitor, but I am come to take his place and to take her," Legoji said.

The old priest to whom he said that laughed. "Many have come for her," he said. "None has yet ever taken her fancy. Her father favored one, but she would not have him. He is here yet. Look out for him!"

Legoji smiled easily and quietly. The old priest found the youth's dignity and self possession more than equal to all his cajolery. He hinted concerning his own learning, but the youth would quietly ask a question reaching beyond all his erudition, until the priest feared the youth made fun of him. He persistently tried to talk to Romperón and Soplón. Romperón answered not a word, but picked up two flagstones and ground them to powder before his eyes. Soplón laughed a little, turned his head toward the priest, and blew him out of the room.

The priest trembled then indeed. Standing outside, he begged Legoji to come to another house—a chief's house—and spend the night.

But Legoji had sized up the construction of the house he was in as he entered; it was just the place for defense. "I have promised to honor this poor man here by spending the night at his home," he replied. "Men tell me Montehcozuma never breaks his word; surely he would despise me if I broke my word. Tell Montehcozuma I will accept from him whatever honors he cares to give me when I have seen him and he me."

The priest left, hurried to Montehcozuma, and related all that had passed. The old chief was much pleased at the answers of the young courtier. Surely he must be a great man of a great people to have so much knowledge. "I will be careful," he said. "Those giants, what are they? What is this youth?" He slept little that night.

Not so the princess. She dreamed all night. This young man so sure of himself—who was he? The priests and chiefs assured her he was half a head taller than the emperor himself. "Fair, jasmine yellow, with big, quiet, all-seeing eyes!" Her dreams were ones that augured well for the young lover.

The next morning Montehcozuma sent his chief priest and the chief of his household with an invitation to his young "friend" to come to the city, bringing his attendants with him.

Legoji accepted gravely, paid his account, and, wishing his host much meat at his house, left with the two messengers, walking between them. Romperón and Soplón followed closely, the former still carrying his bag of round stones. The latter was smiling; whenever he saw maidens getting too close he would send a little wind to the ground to strike just under their skirts and raise them high, or would blow their hair loose and leave them hours of work with *zaatón* brushes getting their hair back in order. If Legoji glanced back, the windy giant appeared as sober as an embalmed body of Guanajuato.

After crossing the long causeway they reached Chapultepec rock and were ushered in to the Great Cacique.

Montehcozuma met him with kindling eyes. His thoughts were these: "Taller by half a head than I, braver than any man I ever saw; quick, quiet, tireless. What a warrior he would be! I must get him for my army! But what is he? No Maya, Zapoteca, Otomiqui, Tototanaca, Mizteca, Tlascalteca, Tihuana, Lascandon, Chomulo, Taramijara, Apache, Tarasco, Comanchi. No, he belongs to no people I have ever seen. If he is a man, there must be men we have never seen yet. Maybe Campos is right and they are all gods." Cold chills ran down his spine.

Legoji stood in a respectful but self-respecting attitude. His eye searched that of the Great Cacique, who had difficulty in meeting the glance.

"Those who are foreigners and come to my court," spoke the Great Cacique, "send word, state their business, and ask my pleasure when they may come. You come unannounced, asking not my permission. I sent a few of my soldiers to meet you and ask what your business was. You slew the commander and routed the force. Why?" The old chief was badly frightened, but the priests must never know it.

"Did not your friend, whom I am proud to call my friend also, send you word of my coming?" Legoji answered, meeting his gaze till the old man's eyes dropped. Another chill ran down his back. Not even the priests knew that.

"Your emissary proved insulting," continued Legoji. "He dared threaten me and began an attack. What would you, Montehcozuma? I fought him fairly and won. His army came after us for shooting him. We fought. Yes, what did you expect, Montehcozuma?"

"Ah, it was you of whom my brother wrote? You came so quickly behind the messenger I could but think you were someone else. I regret this. I am ready to be your friend. But why did you come, now that you are here?" Then Montehcozuma added, "You look like someone I have seen—or dreamed of. Who was it?"

"Which question should I answer first? I know no one you could have seen at all like me." Legoji had totally forgotten the visit of his uncle. "Now, why did I come? I heard you had a beautiful daughter and no son. I thought that if I could be brave enough, strong enough I could win that girl's regard and yours. It is for that I have come."

Xochitl[18] laughed, a gay, happy laugh. No one had ever heard her voice sound so sweet, so deep.

"So that is it?" said the Aztec. Then he went on to tell of the many requirements to be met by the man who should take his daughter from him. "I want," he said, "a man as great or greater than myself; a man who is a warrior ready to lead the people, to fight and to win the fights. He must be a warrior who can slay single-handed the beast whose skin you wear. There are other things. Are you prepared to undergo the tests I will put you to?"

"As for the man who is a warrior," answered Legoji, "did I not best your chieftain, your best fighter? I did that alone. Alone also I slew the jaguar whose skin I wear. You know the first statement to be true; you know the second statement only by my word. Bring your beast and I will slay it as I slew its brother. As for your other tests, put them when you are

[18] Xochitl means *flower;* compare Xochimilco, the famous flower gardens of Mexico.

ready. Meantime may I speak to Xochitl? If she favors me not, my tests may be useless. I want her. Does she want me? That is the question." Legoji turned to look for the princess, but she was gone.

XI. LEGOJI WINS THE NAME OF CUITLAHUAC

Montehcozuma laughed. "Every man coming for my daughter has failed to make the first test. Do you see the great rock up there? Go up this side of the cliff; she will be on top waiting. You may ask her there."

Just then Xochitl and her retinue appeared above waving to them. She seemed to beckon Legoji to come. He stepped back. His eyes met those of Soplón. "Go on," said those eyes.

"That does not seem so difficult!" Legoji said. Turning to Romperón, he added, "Wait with the Great Chief. See no harm comes to him, or me." Then he handed him his robes, his bow and quiver, and stood dressed only in a short apron. To Soplón he said, "Come with me."

He walked to the cliff, ran his eyes over its face a few moments, then trotted back a hundred paces, and ran at it full tilt.

Up, up, up he went a hundred paces before one could realize he had started. The Great Chief caught his breath. On he went. A small projection here, a little niche there into which a foot could be shoved sustained him. Within three or four lengths of the top he faltered. The cliff became overhanging here, and on its smooth sides neither foot nor hand could find support. He lifted his hands, held still a moment, looked up, not down.

Soplón had been watching eagerly. As Legoji's hands were lifted, he coughed. Nothing showed on the smooth face of the rock, but Legoji was lifted up and caught the branch of a tree extending out from the top. The tree bent backward from the breeze as Legoji caught it, and he dropped on the flat, walked to Xochitl. Her maidens crowded around her, but he paid not the slightest attention to them.

"I am come for you," he said.

Xochitl trembled like a flower, her breasts rising and falling in her emotion. She said but two words, "My Chief!"

She was won, and glad to be won; let her hands rest in his, made no attempt to take them from him. Her head was thrown back to almost touch her shoulders.

"I came for you. You shall make me a dish of *menuda!*" said Legoji.

"Yes, my cacique. I will make that and any other dish you may wish. But how did you get up that cliff? It seemed a great wind came with you." Her words were difficult, her heart was beating so. "Oh, I was so afraid you might fall, but I knew you would not fall."

Others of her retinue crowded in. "Wait for Montehcozuma!" said one. Legoji came back to himself. The old chief was coming round the south side of the rock, seated in one hand of Romperón. Soplón followed, bringing the young cacique's headdress, his cloak, and his bow and quiver. Montehcozuma was frightened but doing his best to appear calm and unafraid. The god picked him up, seated him in the palm of his hand, not too gently, and the strong fingers closed on his leg. Some of his retainers had rushed forward with arms to the rescue, but Romperón tightened his fingers and said, "Order them back!"

He realized that with just a little more squeeze there would be another chief of the Aztecs. He quickly ordered: "Back, men! See you not the giant is taking me up the cliff?—something no two of you can do."

Romperón carried him up to Legoji and the princess, set him on the ground before them, walked over and stood behind Legoji. Soplón handed Legoji his apparel, helped him adjust it.

Then Legoji bowed low and said, "I won that test, my lord. Is there any other?"

The old chief was working hard to hide the fear he felt. He never expected Legoji would make it up the cliff. He knew the overhang and believed it could not be mounted from that side. He racked his brain for a test to give Legoji, but could not think of a thing difficult enough. So he said, "One day, one test; another day, another test, my lord!"

This last was said unwittingly. As he had looked at the young chief in his undress, he thought him the most manly being he had ever seen, but when he had put on his finery his dignity was greater than his own.

"Cuitlahuac!" he said. "My home is open to you, but you have not yet won my daughter. He who wins her will win my empire when I am gone."

"Cuitlahuac!" thought Legoji, "a name for a chief; nay, a name for an emperor!"

"My lord," he said, "I must await your pleasure. But Xochitl is mine. Is it not so?" He looked into her eyes for an answer.

"Cuitlahuac, yes!" She repeated the name given by the Great Chief, and said her answer quietly but firmly and with pride. Her bubbling laughter was gone and she faced her father without fear.

Cuitlahuac and his retainers were taken to a stone house designed for and used by nobles. They were treated with the greatest distinction, all their wants supplied. Montehcozuma called and tried to learn from the youth with questions, but found himself, like his priests, answering questions instead of obtaining answers. The youth had some difficulty with the language and made this serve him when he would. Montehcozuma did all he knew to frighten him; but he was cool, quiet and a bit amused apparently. This disconcerted the old chief. He became convinced that Cuitlahuac was half god and half man. He had never before met one who "feared naught in heaven, upon the earth, nor yet in hell!"

Legoji listened attentively to the old chief, of his huntings and his wars. Then he asked him about the priests. This disturbed him greatly and he soon took his leave.

XII. THE TEST OF THE JAGUAR

The next morning at nine Cuitlahuac was before the Great Chief's house with his retainers and was promptly invited into the assembly hall of the nobles. The young chief was refreshed, cool, and determined. Montehcozuma entered just after Legoji; the latter stood with right hand lifted and said, "The Great Chief keeps his word. I want the bride I believe I have fairly won. If not, then I wish the test that will give her to me if I win it."

" 'The Great Chief keeps his word,' " repeated Montehcozuma, "but did I not tell you the cliff was the first test? And after that test did I not say, 'Another day, another test?' "

"I understood that, but at first I understood you to say, 'There is Xochitl, go and take her!' I went. But if the Great Chief does not consider me worthy, I wish to prove that I am. What is the further test?"

"The test now is bravery and endurance. I know that running you can endure, for in coming hither across the sierras you overtook the best runner the cacique of Michoacán could send. But bravery? The Aztecs know no fear. Are you equal to them in that?"

"The cacique knows three of us fought his army and came out best. Campos advised you that four of us fought some thousands of dwarf Guajes. I slew alone the jaguar from which I took this skin. You do not know that but I tell you it is so. I fear no man, nor thing. What is your test, my lord?"

Montehcozuma smiled, called the chief priest and they were talking some time very low. The priest was watching Romperón and Soplón and they were watching the priest. His answers evidently pleased the cacique, for he nodded and called Cuitlahuac to come closer. As the youth approached, the priest stepped back. Soplón coughed a bit; the priest's head hit the flagstone, his feet in the air. He shrieked at Montehcozuma, "No, not that. The gods have heard. Look at me!" And he arose with blood streaming from his face.

Montehcozuma saw what had happened, but did not know how. He was greatly troubled. The sacrifice to the gods of this young noble the gods would not have. He grew pale, but caught his breath and said, "You say you killed the jaguar alone. I have one near here. Are you willing to kill that alone? He is very fierce."

"Is that all, my chief? Come, let us have the sport. You are to loose him thirty paces from me. I will take care of myself."

Xochitl stood up: "If you, my father, turn that beast upon him, I will cast myself to the beast!"

The old cacique was more disturbed. Xochitl, a docile child, defying him? He could not believe it.

But Cuitlahuac stepped over to her. "Have no fear! I am a man! I shall kill him!" Their eyes met. The confidence he had in himself bred confidence in her of him!

"It is well, my father," she said. "Have your way. He will win!"

Cuitlahuac never forgot that. How beautiful is a brave woman! Years afterward he thought of this speech with tender pride, of her love and confidence in him.

"So it will be!" said Montehcozuma and ordered the court adjourned to the *palizada* (the runway) of the tigers.

Xochitl ran to Cuitlahuac, and, pulling his proud head down on her bosom, burst into tears.

Cuitlahuac loosed himself from her very gently. "Have no fear, my woman. I wish your father to see, all to see, how I can fight for you."

Out in the grove adjoining were a stout runway and cages for the great cats, all surrounded by strong trees set close together and four times the height of a man.

Men were sent to drive all the cats back into the cages. The jaguar was surly, as he always was. After delay and difficulty he was finally trapped in a cage alone fronting the runway. The chief then offered Cuitlahuac his choice of weapons, recommending a studded war club, with long sharp obsidian studs. Cuitlahuac had watched that style of club but had wielded one but once. He took it, stepped aside, and swung it several times. He tossed the club over into the stockade. Then, shedding his head-dress and his jaguar skin but retaining his bow and arrows, he vaulted over. "Release your cat!" he cried.

Attendants pulled up the gate. The jaguar jumped outside and ran a short distance; he saw the man, and dropped on his belly with feet lapping the ground. "Look out!" called Xochitl. The jaguar hurled himself upon the man. The youth's time with the unaccustomed club was bad. He swung for the head but missed that and broke a shoulder, and snapped the club short in his hands. The tiger was knocked down by the blow; it screamed fiercely. The youth sprang over him, put ten paces between them, and whirled with an arrow fitted to his bow. As the jaguar sprang again, he let him have the arrow through the heart, ran backward enough to escape the claws, and watched it die.

Men tore open the enclosure, and, Indians as they were, ran to congratulate Cuitlahuac. "He is a cacique, a great cacique! He can fight anywhere and win! He has won the girl, Montehcozuma!" they called.

But jealousy caught the old cacique. He approached the youth, saying, "You have endurance, you are agile, quick and brave, my lord; but you have not won my daughter yet."

Cuitlahuac said, "I believe those are all the qualities you demanded I should have. Xochitl is mine, but, as I said before, I will not take her till the Great Chief is satisfied. I keep my word. What other test have you, my lord?"

Montehcozuma was puzzled. What could he demand now? His people loved Xochitl. She loved the youth. Many were murmuring against him audibly. He looked over toward Popocatepetl, then over to Ajusco vomiting fire and stone. He could see but little of this volcano because of a stone hill raised in the middle of the lake. A thought came to him of something absurd, something that neither the youth nor anyone else could do. He smiled.

XIII. THE ISLAND IN THE LAKE

"You see that stone hill there?" he asked. "It annoys me. You have three days and nights to remove it. Do that and you shall have my daughter at once, be head of my army at once, and head of my empire when I am gone." He laughed a senile cackle and looked at the youth with keen eyes.

Cuitlahuac's eyes dropped, but he stood and held himself proudly erect. He was about to say something which might have been grave when Xochitl gave way to her anger with:

"How absurd! From my former suitors you demanded nothing a man could not do. Why demand that he whom I accept do a thing the gods themselves could not do? That island is of stone, harder even than your heart. I will go with Cuitlahuac whenever he will take me. You cannot kill him unless you destroy me!"

Romperón and Soplón stood looking at the island. One said

something to the other in their own tongue. Legoji heard it, and listened for the answer. He heard that, and, stepping to Montehcozuma, said:

"Very well, in three days and three nights. The fourth day you shall bring Xochitl to me on dry land. If you fail to bring her, I shall come and take her! Then, turning to the people, he raised his voice and said, "You have heard. It is an agreement. I will keep my word; the Great Cacique shall keep his!"

The priests caught Montehcozuma or he would have fallen. Never in his long reign had anyone spoken to him, or of him, in that tone. His people, even his nobles, sympathized with the youth. The Great Cacique saw that, and shivered; then he said in a quiet, even voice, "So it shall be!"

Then to Cuitlahuac he said, "If you have the island leveled in four days and dry land—a causeway across the lake—upon which I can walk, or even a causeway on which to walk with water to my knees, Xochitl shall be brought you and given you at once. You shall at once be the head of my armies, be adopted as my son. If you fail," and here he turned to the priests, "you shall take him to the temple there and rift out his heart, an offering to Huitzilopochtli. I have spoken!"

Cuitlahuac lifted his hand to the emperor, then to the people. Then he walked to Xochitl and said, "Do not fear. What seems impossible shall be done. In four days and nights you shall be mine."

Calling Romperón and Soplón, he walked across to the water, looked over the boats and waved the giants to get into the best. The three shoved off.

As he rowed, Romperón began to sing; Soplón joined in. Their voices were like thunder, and the boat moved so fast they were across the water before the assembled people began to leave the shore they had left.

Only when they reached the island did Cuitlahuac say, "How shall it be done, my great friends?"

"Wait!" both of them answered.

Some poor people lived upon the island. With consideration they were told that Montehcozuma had ordered the island destroyed, that they must leave. The giants were so great the people dared not disobey, but gathered their things, took them into their boats, and left.

Looking over the island, the young prince and his great friends found a live spring of water. Beside it was some dry wood the poor had brought, and to this they helped themselves. There were many fowls on the water. Cuitlahuac shot all they required; they dressed the birds, roasted them, and ate.

Then Romperón arose, stretched his enormous arms and legs, picked up a large stone, and dashed it against the largest rock on the island. The island shook as from an earthquake; a great cloud of dust arose; the rock was broken in many pieces. Romperón picked up the largest of these pieces and dashed them against other stones. There were more quakes and more dust.

Then Soplón stood and sighted a line to the point on the mainland where they had embarked. He filled his lungs and gave a great cough. The ducks he had eaten gave force to his wind and the stones in its path sailed clear across the water and fell on the land close to Montehcozuma's castle. Some piles were left on the island and he repeated his blowings until only three large boulders remained for Romperón.

Cuitlahuac smiled. His boast of dry land for Xochitl in four days did not now seem impossible. "My great brothers," said he, "what shall I do to repay you?"

Both giants laughed and answered, "Have you not already called us 'brothers?' The thing now for us to do is to finish the causeway, destroy the island, and make you captain general of the army and then emperor."

Cuitlahuac laughed again. He got his arrows, killed more ducks, and the giants ate these to make the stones fly.

Montehcozuma and his people saw the flocks of stone cross the water and fall on the shore not far from the palace. Their houses shook as from *temblores*. Great crashes were heard and they saw clouds of dust. They could not imagine what was taking place. Till nightfall the rocks kept coming; the causeway was stretching itself from the mainland towards the island.

After nightfall there was quiet on the island. The whole city was in uproar. "What were these giants? And the cacique with them? Surely they were gods."

Next day as the mists began to lift, crashes were again heard, dust seen; then more rock fell and the causeway grew. Montehcozuma and his nobles watched. Xochitl laughed. At nightfall Montehcozuma looked; from his palace door he could see away down the sides of Ajusco. The island no longer cut off his vision.

When Xochitl saw how much of the island was gone and how the causeway had grown, she realized what was happening; but she was frightened at this great power. Was her lover a god? That frightened her till she remembered how kind were the youth's eyes. "God or man, I love him and he loves me," she said within herself.

Xochitl had many close adherents at court, many whose lives she had saved when her father's temper was bad and he was about to send them to the priests. She called these and told them they must watch the emperor and tell her of anything unusual.

As on the third day Cuitlahuac watched the work progress, he began to fear there would not be enough rock to complete the causeway and maintain the original width. So he ordered that the width be narrowed.

The fish in the lake had become so frightened that they were trying to get out, and he caught all the giants could eat. The giants were tired of duck. Now the gap between the island and the growing causeway was shorter and shorter. Since the stones did not have to fly so far, the work was much easier for Soplón but more difficult for Romperón. Much of the stone had to be broken below the water.

The giants worked till night. Soplón rubbed the fat from the wings of ducks into Romperón's arms, legs, and back. He laughed and joked at Montehcozuma and his nobles. Romperón laughed also. "Maybe some day," he jested, "I will have his head on the ground and smash it with one of those stones."

While two of the party slept at night, the third was always on guard. This night shortly after dark a canoe came to rest and two men walked forward, clapping their hands, to the fire. Cuitlahuac met them and asked what they would have.

"We come from Xochitl," said the men. "She says to keep sharp watch; there is something going on. What it is she does not know, but a number of prisoners have been loosed, and they have talked to the Great Cacique. She expects you to be attacked before dawn."

The two joined Cuitlahuac's forces and had some of their fish. The fire was banked to cut off all light. Cuitlahuac told the giants to sleep, that he and these men would watch. About midnight Cuitlahuac heard a light splash in the water to their right and investigated. One man came out of the water, then another, and another until there were many. He put his hand over Soplón's mouth, slipped the other under his head, and shook it gently, woke him without sound.

"Look!" he whispered. "Montehcozuma is about to lose. He sends those to murder us. Blow them into his castle!"

Montehcozuma a half-mile away was awakened by the bodies of the men he had sent crashing into his castle; one fell in the princess's chamber. The whole castle was in an uproar. Lights were brought and the dead were counted and recognized. Montehcozuma found not one was missing; all were dead. The bodies were picked up and taken to their homes. Montehcozuma was frightened! He knew he had sent the men to their death. "What is the use?" he asked himself. "I cannot fight them. They are gods and know what we think before one speaks. I am only a man. If the young chief wants my daughter, he will take her and I cannot prevent him. I hope that her children will be as he is, half god and half man."

After the blowing away of the attackers, the two secret messengers stole back to the city and the giants went to sleep again. Just as the dawn began to paint the eastern sky a faint red, Soplón yet asleep turned on his side and gave a tremendous cough. Romperón was directly before him and he was blown far out into the lake. Cuitlahuac ran to a boat, jumped in, rowed swiftly to the place where his great friend had sunk. He found nothing above the waters. Meantime, Soplón, awakened by his cough, found Romperón gone and realized what had happened. In the dim light he watched Cuitlahuac. He saw that his chieftain found nothing on the waters. Then he threw his hands up high above his head, bent over so that his mouth faced the ground, and gave a thundering cough. The island sprang down, then rebounded. The rebound threw Soplón far out into the deep. Cuitlahuac, who had been attracted by the thundering sound of the cough, saw him go through the air, saw him splash into the waters. He hurried his boat to the spot. The body did not come up. Cuitlahuac waited and watched, but nothing appeared in either place where the giants had gone down. Slowly then he rowed back to where the island had been, no part of it visible now. He got out of the boat and sat on the end of the causeway and thought.

XIV. THE PRINCESS WON. THE END OF CUITLAHUAC

While he sat there in the misty light, he saw Montehcozuma appear on the other end of the causeway, his hand lifted, waiting. When Montehcozuma saw that he was recognized, he waved encouragement to Cuitlahuac and walked back to shore. There he called his nobles and the priests, called Xochitl. He told them the causeway was complete. He walked forward holding the girl's right hand in his left, his own right hand lifted. They saw how the island was vanished. As they proceeded, Ajusco shone in all its splendor and spouted an enormous flame, seeming to add glory to the event.

The old cacique was very tender to Xochitl. "Your lover has won," he said. "I am taking you to him. May you have many children, and may the gods fight for you as they fight for him!"

Xochitl put her arms about the old man, thanked him with her head pillowed against his breast. "May my husband be as great as you," she said.

Montehcozuma turned to his nobles and priests with these words: "The gods are upon the earth. Cuitlahuac is high in their favor and they have come to us. There is another which will come, the White God—Quetzalcoahuatl!"

He ordered the preparations of games and feasts; he ordered all his prisoners freed. He did all he knew how to make everyone else happy, but he could not be happy himself. The

Aztecs walked on, and as they neared the place where the island had been they saw Cuitlahuac walking alone to meet them.

He had gathered himself together from the sorrow at the loss of his great friends. Now as the royal party approached, he dropped his bow and arrow and lifted his right hand. His sorrow was great, but he loved the girl and could feel his pulse quicken at her approach. A smile came to his face.

Montehcozuma said, "My son, here is your bride. Take her."

Cuitlahuac held out his hands and the girl sprang into his arms.

"Where are your great companions?" asked Montehcozuma.

"They left me at dawn today."

"Where did they go?"

"That I know not. They came to me when I needed them. Now I do not need them. Perhaps they may come again when I do need them."

Xochitl was the only being who ever learned from him where they went or how. The lava from Ajusco flowed down into the lake and covered the place where the bodies lay.

Only after the conquistadores had come and Cortez had usurped everything, did Cuitlahuac fail to obey the old chief. Then he threw over his allegiance to the Great Cacique and drove the invaders from the city. Cuitlahuac was everywhere in that battle, but he was so badly wounded he was unable to follow up the victory he had won.

CANTO DEL NIÑO PERDIDO

Edited by MARY R. VAN STONE AND E. R. SIMS

This is an old New Mexican folk play that probably originated three hundred years ago when the priests taught the Indians and common people by means of pantomimes and plays illustrating Bible stories. In New Mexico, every year at Christmas time, every little village and community of any size will be giving "Los Pastores" or "Nuestra Señora de Guadalupe." Some years ago in Santa Fe the Mexican folk began "Los Pastores" a month before Christmas, giving it every night until after New Year's day. In the State Museum at Santa Fe are a dozen different versions of "Los Pastores" collected from different places, some of which have been very carefully translated. Only one version of "El Niño Perdido" is to be found here, although other versions are in Albuquerque. It is possible that, being a Penitente play, it has not been encouraged as has "Los Pastores."

In February, early in Lent of 1933, it was produced in a suburb of Taos about a mile from the plaza. The stage was a large vacant corner lot, dozens of pine trees about six feet high having been set up in rows across the lot to represent a forest. At one end of this long narrow lot was hung a white sheet for a back, or side, drop, and the actors went behind this when they left the stage. The top of a barn covered with hay in an adjoining lot was the gallery where a large part of the audience sat, and along the side of the barn two immense logs were the reserved seats. Opposite this barn were parked cars on the running boards of which people sat, some standing on the fence to get a better view.

At about two o'clock the official prompter came from behind the curtain and announced the play with a summary of the story—that of the Child Jesus when he was twelve years old having been lost for three days and finally found in the temple talking with the "Doctors." Then from behind the curtain came the sound of the Penitente flute, and a chorus of men's voices in the first *letra*. At every change of scene throughout the play a *letra* was sung by the chorus, accompanied by the flute. The wandering of Mary and Joseph through the forest searching for the Child filled up most of the first act, but the Rich Man and his conversations with his clownish servant gave the necessary touch of comedy. The Rich Man was seated at a small table near the curtain at one end of the "stage" and at the other end sat the six Doctors around a larger table, all dressed in black cassocks such as are worn by choristers. In the middle of the stage sat three men in black dresses and long black veils who comforted Mary and Joseph, and later on the Child, in their sad wanderings. After the feasting by the Rich Man on much wine (pink soda-pop) and after the lamentations of Mary and Joseph, came an intermission, when the chorus sang a long "Miserere," accompanied by the flute. This was undoubtedly one of the Penitente songs to be heard during Lent.

In the second act, after a short *letra* by the chorus, the Child appeared wandering through the forest, telling of the agonies to come and of the cruel punishments predicted for him. The part was enacted by a small boy not over twelve years old, who had a lovely face and wore a long black wig. He had a remarkable memory, his lines filling several pages of the manuscript, which we followed closely. The prompter repeated or sang the lines along with all the actors, seemingly not disconcerting them in the least. The Angel appeared at the end, over the top of the curtain, where he sat perched on a ladder, apparently. He was dressed in a white lace dress, with crown and wings. Mary was dressed in a light blue evening dress in the latest style, with high-heeled slippers and a long blue veil. She did not look cold, but the Child's teeth chattered so that they had to put a coat on him over his white robes. The childlike sincerity of the people was evident in every line they spoke and listened to, and the action was at all times dignified and in keeping with the religious character of the play.

El Niño, la Virgen, and San José sing all of their lines to respective tunes. All the other characters speak their lines. The *letras* are sung by a chorus of men's voices behind the scenes.—M. R. V. S.

Working from a typewritten copy of a manuscript does not leave much play for the imagination. The condition of this particular manuscript of the *auto* is an excellent example of how oral transmission can garble things; particularly, when abstruse language is understood. There is abundant internal evidence of scholarly origin: classical allusions, language, the thesis itself, the presence of a comic element, and other points that need not be mentioned. The verse form, *romance* predominating, with some *décimas,* is further proof of the antiquity of the *auto*.

Mrs. Van Stone and I have tried to reproduce faithfully the manuscript of the State Museum of New Mexico. We have full knowledge of its shortcomings; many passages are meaningless; in places, entire lines have been lost. Perhaps some reader may be able to supply these portions. Some passages of the translation are hazards at an attempt to make sense out of what is senseless.

Dr. R. L. Stephenson of the University of Texas has been of great assistance in restoring some passages to their proper form and in interpreting a number of readings that seemed unintelligible.

Mr. A. L. Campa of the University of New Mexico generously furnished readings from his manuscripts and offered other valuable suggestions. Passages in Spanish adopted from his versions have been enclosed in brackets. Since Mr. Campa is preparing a study of the early religious drama in New Mexico, it would have been obviously unfair to him to adopt more corrections than are absolutely necessary. His study, which will include this *auto,* will appear shortly.

In the English translation parentheses enclose additions necessary to make the meaning clearer to those who do not understand Spanish.—E. R. S.

El Niño Perdido

The Lost Child

Letra

Chorus

All the *letras,* or choruses, except as indicated, are sung to this tune.

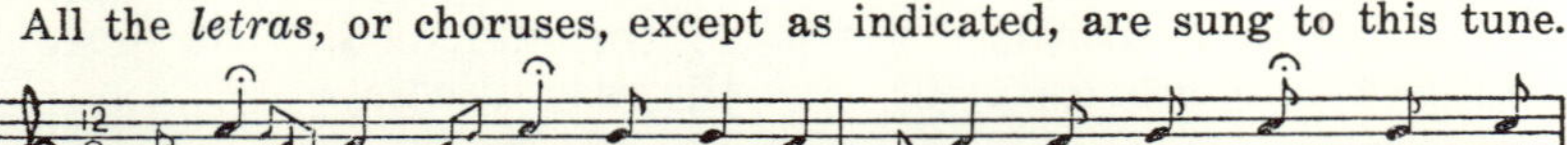

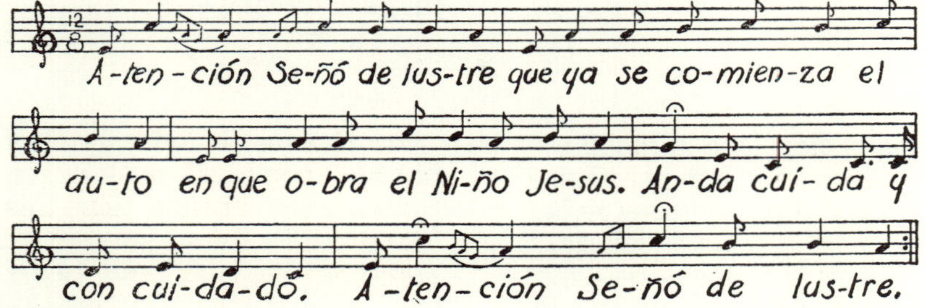

Atención, señor de lustre,
Que ya se comienza el auto
En que obra el niño Jesús;
Ande quedo y con cuidado.

Attention, gentle sirs. Now begins the play in which the Child Jesus appears; move quietly and with care.

Felix

¿Qué hacen aquí tan despacio
En cuestiones divertidos
Molestando al auditorio?
Voy que estoy muy aburrido,
Vamos, que se haga un coloquio,
Que esta plaga ha prevenido,
Que es auto sacramental
Que se hace al niño perdido.
Gustaremos de estos versos
Y después que se haga el vino,
De sopapillas y tamales
Con manteca de cochino
Que han matado en la casa
De un obsequioso vecino;
Y después de una larga cena
Que se forme un fandanguillo
Y que bailen chiles verdes
Y la danza de monitos
Y que traigan otros juguetes
Menos los apretoncitos,
Porque estos no se hacen aquí,
Sólo allá en los alamitos.

Felix

What do you here so calmly in idle talk, molesting the audience? Take care or I shall become vexed; come, let the play begin, which this crowd has prevented; it is a religious play dedicated to the lost child. We shall enjoy these verses and then let wine be served, and cakes and *tamales* with drippings of pork. A pig has been slaughtered by a generous neighbor, and after a plentiful supper let the *fandango* be danced and the *chiles verdes* perform and the dance of the *monitos* (mimics). Let other games be played, except the *apretoncitos,* for these are not played here, only yonder among the poplars.

Letra

¡Vamos, ándale! que es hora,
Y para que nazca el sol
Nos alumbra su farol,
La más refulgente aurora.

Chorus

Come, hurry! The hour has come. Announcing the birth of the sun, comes the herald, the rosy dawn.

Carrasco

En el cielo está la gloria;
Todos, venid con presteza,
Que no a todas horas se halla
En el mundo esta belleza.
Hoy, si la pluma descoto,
Hoy, sí profunda de ameno,
O la ciencia de un patriarca
O sí mi lengua ayudara
Quien es el presbítero
Don Luis mas él . . . .
A quien sus dones [ensalzan]
Bien pudiera y bien quisiera
Prevenir sus prendas raras;
Pero su mucha modestia
Toda mi atención embarga,
Como también los justicias
Que a fuerza de sus constancias,
Solicitud y trabajo
Se llegan las alabanzas.
Yo soy nuevo en el oficio
Y no estoy examinado
Hasta que no me examine
Cristo, San Pedro y San Pablo,
Y los cuatro Evangelios
Que el Señor traía a su lado.
Voy a repetir el verso
Y a darles el parabién.
Dios les conserve la vida
Señores y a mí también.

Carrasco

In Heaven is where glory belongs; come, all, with haste, for it is not always that this treasure is found on earth. Today if I gave free rein to my pen skilled in compliment, there would issue the wisdom of a patriarch or praise for the presbyter, Don Louis. Anyone might well bespeak his grace and rare gifts. But his modesty forbids my just praise, as do the officials whose faithfulness, solicitude, and labor well merit praise. I am new in this rôle. I have not been tried, nor will be until I am put to the proof by Christ, St. Peter, St. Paul and the four Evangelists whom He had at His side. I shall repeat the verse and bid them (the actors) welcome. May God keep them and me as well.

Letra *Chorus*

In the *letras* that follow, the last line, as in this, is repeated instead of the first line, as above.

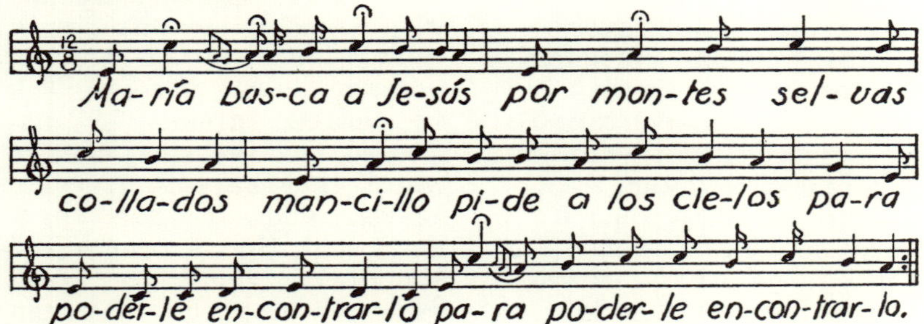

María busca a Jesús
Por montes, selvas, collados;
Auxilio pide a los cielos
Para poder encontrarlo.

Mary seeks Jesus through mountains, forests, and hills; she implores the aid of heaven in order to find Him.

Virgen *Virgin*

This tune is for all lines ascribed to the Virgin.

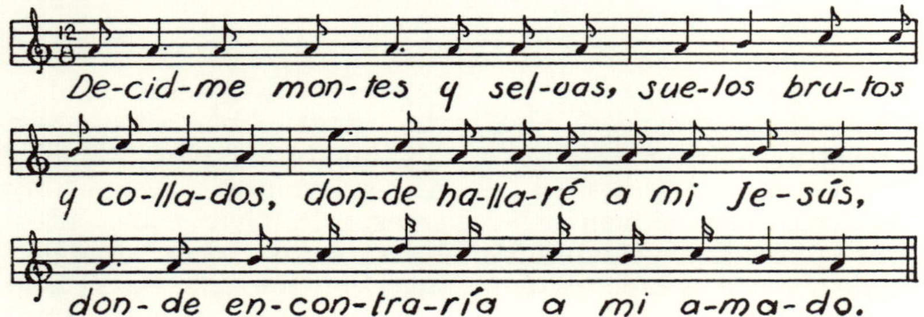

Decidme montes y selvas,
Suelos brutos y collados:
¿Dónde hallaré a mi Jesús?
¿Dónde encontraría a mi amado?
No es la moneda perdida
La que busca mi cuidado;
Es el único tesoro
Y vale mucho [su hallazgo].
Dulce amor, gloria de mi alma,
¿Dónde te me has ausentado?
¿A dónde podré encontrar

Tell me, forests, mountains, wild desert places, where will I find my Jesus? Where can I find my beloved? It is not a lost coin that my care seeks; it is the only treasure and its recovery is worth much. Tell me, my love, glory of my soul, where have you gone? Where can I find your two sovereign eyes? Would you that I end

Tus dos soles soberanos?
¿Quieres que acabe la vida
Con el penetrante dardo
Que de mi vista quitó
La claridad de tus rayos?
¿Por qué me has enriquecido
Con tus divinos regalos,
Con tu infancia y con tan sólo
Me habías de llevar temprano?
Decidme, cielo divino,
Si acaso han desagradado
De los pecados del mundo
Y a la gloria se han tornado.
Aquella brasa encendida,
Aquel Mongibel nevado,
Vomitando llamas nuevas
En visiones se han citado.
Ah! que le busque con ansiez,
Como está profetizado,
Aquel tiempo [perentorio]
Que sería crucificado.
¡Ay de mí! si con el cetro
Los rigores fueren dados
De su padre, el rey Herodes,
Al sucesor herodiano.

my life with the piercing shaft that took the light of your look from my sight? Why have you enriched me with your divine gifts, with your infancy, if you were to take them away so soon? Tell me, heaven divine, if, displeased at the sins of the world, they have returned to heaven above? That burning brand, that snow-covered Mongibel, vomiting fresh flames, in prophecies has been told of. Ah! let men seek Him anxiously, since this inevitable crucifixion has been foretold. Woe is me, if with the scepter the cruelties of the father, King Herod, should be transmitted to his hereditary successor.

Que un dañado corazón
Induce al apacionado
A mostrar delirio nativo
Para vengar sus agravios.
¡Ay Jesús! ¡Ay mi bien!
¡Qué afectos tan encumbrados
Desde ahora y cuando te tuve
Recién nacido en mis brazos!
De los pastores servidos,
De los reyes adorados,
Y de las celestes tropas
Como a su Dios venerado.
¡Qué contrario es mi pesar
Al gusto que tuve cuando
Simón te profetizó
Por el Mesías deseado!
¡Qué desconsuelo al consuelo
Aunque en temores mezclado,
Cuando huyendo para Egipto
Te llevaba en mis regazos!

For an evil heart induces the angry one to show his innate rage in avenging his grievances. Jesus! My treasure! What noble affections have been showered upon you since the time I held you new-born in my arms! Served by the shepherds, worshiped by kings, venerated as their God by the celestial throngs! How far removed is my present sorrow from the joy I felt when Simeon proclaimed you for the long-desired Messiah. How far the present grief from the peace I felt, although it was mingled with fear, when in our flight to Egypt I held you in my lap.

Contigo, dulce amor mío,
Las penas me son regalos;
Sin ti no puedo hallar gusto;
Fuera de mí puedes darlo.
Si acaso por mi descuido
Yo a tu servicio he faltado,
Corrige, Señor, tu esclava,
Pues por mí andas a los sabios.
Y así, no me des tormentos
En tan exhibidos grados
Cuando a usar de tu clemencia
Estás siempre acostumbrado.
Reciba, a donde quiera
Que esté mi bien ocultado,
De mi doloroso pecho
Los suspiros que he exhalado.
Que como intimo, debe
Andar con su cetro buscando
Como hambriento a las alturas
Y a su celeste pasto.
Aunque llovido del cielo
Vino en misteriosos grados,
Que yo en tanto que no lo hallo
Viviré en continuo llanto;
Sola, triste y sin consuelo
Sin alivio ni descanso.
Y si por ser su indigna madre
[A El puedo suplicarlo]
Déme licencia, Dios mío,
Para poder (lo) encontrarlo.

With you, my sweet love, my sorrows turn to joys; without you, I find no happiness; away from me, you may bestow it. If perhaps neglect has led me to fail in your service, chasten, Lord, your slave, since through me you go in search of the wise. And thus torment me no longer in so manifest a way, whereas you are always accustomed to show clemency. May my treasure receive, wherever He may be concealed, the sighs that I have breathed from my sorrowing breast. For, as I suspect, with his scepter he must be seeking as one thirsting for the heights of his heavenly pasture. Although from heaven descended, He came by mysterious steps, and I while He is not found shall live in continual grief, alone, sad, without comfort, relief or rest. And if being His unworthy mother permits me to implore Him, grant, Oh God, that I may find Him.

Letra

San José en su pecho siente
La ausencia de su querido,
Sale en congojas y penas
A buscar su bien perdido.

Chorus

Saint Joseph in his heart mourns the loss of his beloved; in grief and sorrow he goes out to seek his lost treasure.

San José *Saint Joseph*

All lines for San José are sung to this tune.

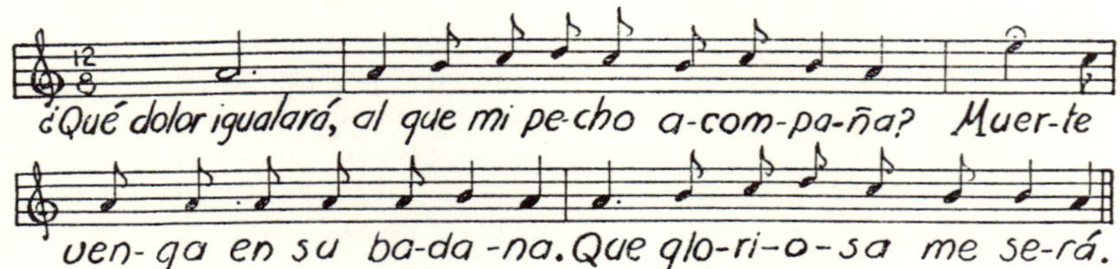

¿Qué dolor igualará
Al que mi pecho acompaña?
Muerte, venga en su badana,
Que gloriosa me será;
Pues ninguno perderá
El bien que traigo perdido,
Desgraciado en sumo he sido
Cuanto en sumo fuí dichoso,
Y no espero tener gozo
Hasta hallar a mi querido.
Perdió Jacobo a José
Por la fraterna traición
En triste lamentación
Pasó el tiempo y ya se ve
Pues la pérdida no fué
Tan grande, y a buena luz
Saltó a los ojos un flux
Por lo mucho que lloró.
¿Cómo no he de llorar yo
La ausencia de mi Jesús?
Tan solamente en pensar
Si mi tibieza ha causado
Haberle desagradado
Llega el tiempo de espirar.
¿Cómo podré restaurar
Prendas de precio infinito
Si le perdió mi delito?
Este es mi mayor tormento
En que cada instante siento
Del corazón el conflicto.
El ver que mi amada esposa
Y castísima María
Ni de noche ni de día
Un instante no reposa;
Cual si fuera mariposa

What sorrow can equal that which my breast holds? O Death, all draped in white, come! How glorious that will be for me, for no one will lose the treasure that I have lost. My present misfortune can only be measured by my former good fortune; I can not again look for happiness until I find my beloved. Jacob lost his son Joseph through the treachery of his brothers; in sorrow he spent his days; though his loss was not so great as mine, yet there flowed from his eyes a river of tears. Why then shall I not weep for the absence of my Jesus? The mere thinking that my carelessness may have caused his displeasure brings me near to death. How then can I restore treasures of infinite worth if mine is the blame for their loss? My greatest torment is to feel remorse struggling in my breast. To see my beloved spouse, the most pure Mary, day and night without repose is my greatest torment, in which I feel the conflict at each moment in my heart. My beloved spouse, the most pure Mary, night and day without

(Cual caviló el Faraón)
No encuentra en su corazón
[La paz; de Jesús el vuelo]
Por instantes, por desvelo
Turbó su imaginación.
Dudoso estoy en un tomo
Si esta pérdida habrá sido
Por su industria o mis descuidos,
Y no puedo hallar asomo
De cualquier manera tomo
Un medio para encontrarlo
Que hasta el último, si vale.
Que ni la tribulación,
Cuchillo, persecución
[Me impide para encontrarle:]
Dulce Jesús por quien vivo,
Pues que llegué a merecer
[Que cual autor de tu ser,]
Me quisieses putativo,
Dáme aquel glorioso alivio
Que pretende mi cuidado.
Seré de tu ciencia guiado
Que con tal felicidad
Será mi infelicidad
Todo pesar revocado.

an instant's repose, as if she were a butterfly, or the hesitating Pharaoh, does not find in her heart peace; the flight of the child Jesus every moment disturbs her mind. I know not if this loss has been through His desire or through my neglect. I can find no trace, whatever means I employ to find Him. Even to the uttermost I am disposed to seek if permitted, for neither tribulation, death, nor persecution can prevent me from finding Him. Sweet Jesus, for whom I live, since I have merited being called your father, give me that glorious surcease from sorrow that my anxiety seeks. I will be guided by your wisdom, for with such happiness my every sorrow will be removed.

Letra

Ostentando su grandeza
Sale como vengativo
Y le negará el sustento
Al niño que anda afligido.

Chorus

Displaying his grandeur there will come one who revengeful will deny sustenance to the distressed child.

Rico

Ya es a las dos, pero el criado
Como así poco advertido
Sin aparato a la mesa.
¿A esta hora tanto descuido?
Por la corona del rey, villano,
Ya corresponde un castigo
Y bien mereces mi enojo
Pero los días que diviso
De pascuas, has de agradecerme.

Rich Man

It is already two o'clock, but the lazy servant has not set the table. Such carelessness at this hour? By the king's crown, villain, punishment is due you and you well deserve my anger. You can thank the approaching festive days for my clemency.

Carrasco

¡Ay! su mercé no habrá sabido
Que un fuerte dolor de muela
Me ha echado a perder el juicio,
Y salí a ver si topaba
Quien me echase un exorcismo,
Y avergonzado volvíme
De la casa del vecino.
Pero por mi güena suerte
En mí el refrán se ha cumplido
Y lo vine a hallar en casa
De un asesino afligido.

Carrasco

Ah, your grace cannot know how a terrible toothache has driven me mad and I went out to find some one who could give me a charm, but I have returned ashamed from the house of our neighbor. But my good fortune willed that the proverb should be fulfilled, and I have found it in the house of a wretched murderer.[1]

Rico

Malicioso es el villano,
A hacerme el desentendido.
No os entiendo que decís.

Rich Man

The rascal is shrewd, but I will pretend that I have not understood—I do not understand what you are saying.

Carrasco

Pese el cornudo que me hizo
Pimienta; chitón,señor;
Y no hallo el menor alivio
Que me ha güelto el dolor.

Carrasco

Bad luck to the cuckold who deceived me. Silence, sir, I do not find relief; the pain has returned.

Rico

Que toquen; ande pícaro.

Rich Man

Let the music begin; hurry, rascal.

Carrasco

Señores, jamás se ha visto
Que un hombre con tantas
barbas
Se haga, como éste, chiquito.
Voto al perro del demonio
Que el mundo no tendrá oficio
Más ilustre que es servir;

Carrasco

Sirs, no one has ever seen a man with so much beard act a child as this one does. I swear by the devil's dog that there is no better calling than service; and more so under a man of importance. These rich men

[1] The proverb: "The remedy is found in the house of a murderer" (or, of a hangman).

Y más si es un hombre [altivo].
Estos, digo, nunca piensan
En la gloria ni en el juicio.
Toda su gloria es comer, beber;
Nunca dan limosna aunque es
su oficio
Y siempre desprecian [al pobre].
[Cantar, músicos; cuidado
Que nadie les haga ruido.]

never think of glory nor of judgment. All their glory is eating and drinking; they never give alms, although it is their duty, and they scorn the poor and unfortunate. Sing, musicians; let every one be careful not to make any noise.

Letra

Quien tiene dinero, tiene
Los imposibles vencidos:
Los reyes lo han menester
Los pobres buscan su auxilio.

Chorus

He who has money has the impossible overcome; kings have need of it and the poor seek its aid.

Carrasco

Cálale de arriba abajo,
Dirán que soy adivino
Y que un peon no divertía
Y que el perro era un pollino.

Carrasco

Strip him from top to bottom. They will say that I am a prophet, that a peon did not amuse, and that the dog was a donkey.

Celio

Eso no.

Celio

Not that.

Carrasco

¡Que lindo!
Entre bobos anda el juego,
Y este bobón divertido
No escapó como él dice;
Escapó con sus navíos.
Estas son más que sirenas,
Apriétenle otro tantito.

Carrasco

Fine! The game is between fools, and this big happy fool did not escape as he says. He escaped with his ships. These are more than sirens; bear down a little more.

Rico

Que repitan esa letra
U otra en el mismo sentido.

Rich Man

Let them repeat that chorus or another with the same sense.

Carrasco

Sin sentido has de quedar
Y bien chupado burrico.

Carrasco

You are going to be left without sense and a well-bled donkey as well.

Letra

La soga trae arrastrando
Y en la garganta el cuchillo
El que no condescendió
Con la voluntad de un rico.

Letra

He who does not bow to the will of a rich man drags his own rope (to the gallows) and has a knife at his throat.

Carrasco

Se habrán visto picarones
Que tal hayan discurrido?
El juicio me han de quitar
Y si no quemo mis libros.

Carrasco

Has anyone ever seen rogues that would say such things? They are going to drive me crazy or, if not, I will burn my books.

Rico

De esta cadena de oro
Sean los músicos servidos.

Rich Man

Let the musicians be pleased to accept this gold chain.

Carrasco

Lo que si el céfiro sopla
Se lo han de llevar ungido,
Los cascos se le han de hinchar
Hasta dar el estallido.
Entro yo a probar fortuna.
Señor, no habrá un dobloncillo?
Yo también compongo versos
Que me gustará mucho decirlos.

Carrasco

This time the sighing zephyrs have brought them a reward; their heads are going to swell until they burst. I am going to try my luck. Sir, isn't there a single *dobloncillo* for me? I also compose verses, and it will give me pleasure to recite them.

Rico

Perversos serán, caballo,
Pero, sin embargo, dílos.

Rich Man

Perverse ones they will be, horse. However, say them.

Carrasco

Son versos cómicos
De mi [numen] discurridos,

Carrasco

They are comic verses recited from memory, for when

Que en parándose la vena
Es un caudaloso río.
Molpe, Telepio, allá blasona;
Cada una sirena es remolona,
Ave de rapiña, pies y garras
Que con sonoras voces bizarras
Que a dos bobos se embargan
De tal modo a que libraran
A los otros, le dan con todo.
Pocos Ulises al presente topo;
O yo estoy cierto, señores,
O yo estoy loco.
Porque en jurando la bendición
De mis calzones que los demás
Los veo por ahí a montones.

the stream has stopped it becomes a turbulent river. Molpe, Telepio, show your worth; all sirens (muses) are indolent, birds of prey, feet and claws that with strange sonorous voices prevent two fools from freeing the others. At present I rarely meet a Ulysses. This is true, sirs, or I am mad. * * * *

Rico

Tu malicia he penetrado
Por lo tanto lo he advertido
Que junto con el perdón
Tome el doblón que has pedido.

Rich Man

I have understood your insinuation; therefore I have advised that along with the pardon you will take the doubloon you have asked for.

Carrasco

Doblón, doblón, en mis manos
Cuando el contagio me ha cogido
Se siente el céfiro soplar
Me andan a tirar el caído.

Carrasco

A doubloon, a doubloon in my hands? When the contagion has seized me, I feel the south wind blow. It comes to take away my melancholy.

Rico

Que cante, Lelio.
Andá vos, malicioso,
Traé el vino.

Rich Man

Let them sing, Lelio; you, rascal, go and bring the wine.

Lelio

Y para que esté más lucido
Y a mí me den buen concepto
Las gentes que aquí han venido,
Yo en el coloquio he pensado
Que se le ponga la mesa a un rico,

Lelio

To add something to the appearance of the stage and so that the people who have come here will give me a good report, I have arranged to have

Y que tal me la pusiera yo
Si me deja Carrasquillo.

a table placed for the rich man. And such would I place for myself if Carrasco would allow.

Letra

Nadie se oponga al poder
De un poderoso que es rico;
Halla mucho en que vengarse
Cuando se mira ofendido.

Chorus

Let no one oppose the power of a rich man in authority, for he finds many a way to take revenge when he fancies himself offended.

Carrasco

Cuando la cabeza es mala
Los miembros dan en lo mismo;
Mi amo bebe y yo también
He de gustar de un traguito;
Sona, que bien que me sabes,
Que desde hoy para siempre afirmo
Que el oficio de copero
Es honrado beneficio.
Mientras Dios me dé dinero
No he de dejar este oficio.

Carrasco

When the source becomes disordered, the members suffer in like degree. My master drinks and I shall also take a sip. Ah! How good you taste. Henceforth I shall always affirm that the office of cupbearer is a place of honor and as long as God gives me money I shall not forsake it.

Rico

Con primor habla la letra,
Que el caso es visto
Que nunca falta materia
Al pobre para un delito.
A vos confiado en derecho
De creencias poco advertido
Quiso resistirse acaso
Un pundonoroso y altivo
Perdiendo en un todo, fama,
Vida, creencia y señorío.
Antes de esto en otra vez
Se puede probar lo mismo.
Ahimelech, el sacerdote
Con otros ochenta y cinco,
Que estos pueden ser testigos,

Rich Man

The chorus expresses the matter aptly, for the case is self-evident, that there is never lacking a way to put a poor man in the wrong. Trusting in his rights and little skilled in practice, an honorable and proud man tried to oppose you (a rich man), thereby losing his honor, life and rank. Many an example of this may be taken from olden times.

Ahimelech, the priest, with eighty-five others can also be witnesses. Solely because Ahi-

Tan sólo por socorrer
Ahimelech y compasivo
A David cuando de Saul,
El rey, anduvo perseguido,
Doeg de Idumea en la nación
Como probado y valido,
Luego que vió la traición
Le trajo al rey el aviso.
Murió al fin Ahimelech
Y los demás como he dicho,
Librando solo Abiatar
Los rigores del cuchillo.
Urías, otro caballero,
Más soldado que marino
En el tiempo en que pensó
Subir, cayó al precipicio.
Mucho os pudiera decir
En la materia acaecido
Común y particular
Que por notorio lo omito.

melech had pity upon David when he was pursued by King Saul, Doeg, an Idumean by birth, when he witnessed the treason, as a loyal and brave man immediately brought warning to the king. Ahimelech died and all the rest, as I have said; only Abiathar escaped the cruelty of the knife. Uriah, another noble, more soldier than sailor, in the time when he thought to rise, fell into the abyss. Much could I tell you of the same nature, both general and particular, which, because it is notorious, I shall omit.

Letra

Sale el cordero inocente
A meditar su pasión;
En fuego y amor ardiente
Se inflama su corazón.

Chorus

The innocent Lamb comes to meditate upon his suffering. His heart is ignited with the flames of love.

El Niño

The Child

The Niño sings all his lines to this tune.

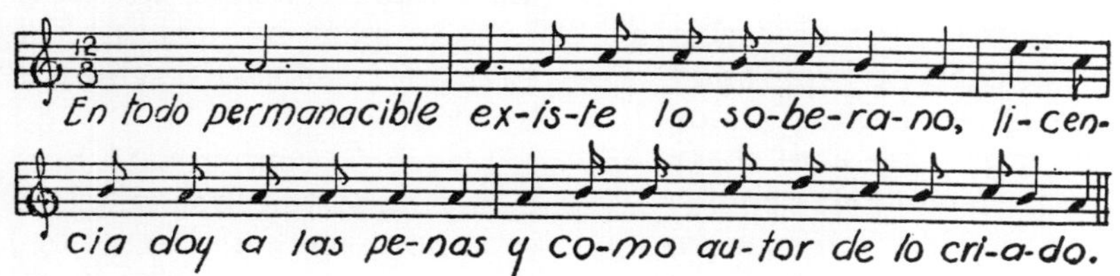

Por mas que me mira Dios
Siendo a un mismo tiempo
humano
He de entrar por el conducto
De conflictos y trabajos.
En todo permanecible

Although God looks upon me with favor, yet since I am at the same time human, I shall enter upon the way of conflict and labor. In all the durable there exists sovereignty; I al-

Existe lo soberano
Licencia doy a las penas;
Y como autor de lo criado
Fórmese la tempestad
Con volcanes desatados;
Llegue la sed, llegue el hambre,
Calor, tristeza y cansancio.
Aquel que nace a la vida
A ganar premios y [lauros]
Se ha de armar de pentencia
Que es el modo de ganarlos.
De Getsemaní, el huerto,
Esto está bien celebrado,
Pues es licor de mi sangre
Y sudor donde regalo.
No vengo a ver la hermosura
Que le dió mi franca mano
Cuando de lo pura y bella
Sin igualdad se ha ausentado.
No quiero del Rey Señor
Dulces montes y triunfando
Si el ave de gracia llena
Por mi ausencia está llorando.
¡Ay, María y querida madre!
Yo siento el dolor entre ambos;
El que de mi padre José
Al corazón ha llegado.
Mas es preciso cumplir
El ministerio de quien me ha
enviado;
Vine al mundo de lamentos
De mi padre destinado.
Maestro soy y como maestro
He de enseñar [apurando,]
Que la enseñanza [mejor]
[Es la palabra aquí obrando.]
Quiero contemplar aquí
De mi mente el primer paso,
Que el mal por malo que sea
Prevenido es menos malo.
Enristra la lanza airosa
Y montando en el caballo
Poco a poco reconoce
De la campaña los daños,
Y cuando llega a pelear

low grief (to beset me). As author of all creation I allow the tempest to form of unloosed volcanoes. Let thirst come and famine and sorrow and weariness. He who would gain reward and win laurels of life, let him gird himself with penitence, the only means of gaining them. This garden of Gethsemane is renowned, since here my blood and sweat I bequeath (to mankind). I do not come to see the beauty given by my free hand after it has parted from purity and peerless beauty.

I do not seek from the King pleasant woods nor triumphs if the dove abounding in grace mourns my absence. Oh Mary, my beloved mother! I mourn for the grief of you both, for that which has pierced the heart of my father Joseph. But it is necessary to fulfill the ministry of Him who sent Me. I came to the world of sorrows, sent of my Father. I am a teacher, and as a teacher I am to teach by draining the [cup], for the best teaching is by example.

I wish to contemplate here in my mind the first step, for evil, however evil it may be, foreseen is less so. The (captain) takes the graceful lance and, mounting his horse, little by little perceives the damages of the campaign; and when the battle is joined he has much gained, for darts fore-

Tiene mucho adelantado
Que los dardos prevenidos
Tienen mucho en siendo dardos.
Bien que todo lo que sea
Dolores, penas y agravios
No pretende haber ninguno
Alivio, gusto y descanso.
Aqui fué la noche triste
Que ahora mi padre está orando
En recuerdo de mi cruz.
Gustaré el caliz amargo
Aquí por rios de coral
Mixtos en sudores [claros]
Serán las cándidas flores
Claveles ensangrentados.
Este es el lugar en que
Un profundo sueño he dado;
En vez de guardia estarán
Mis discípulos amados.
Aquí el alevoso Judas
Traidor con asco y falso
[Lleno de avaricia y saña]
Me entregará a mis contrarios.
¡O envidia! una serpiente y fea,
Astuta, atroz sin reparo
No tendrás fin hasta el mundo
No se ve ya finado.
A mí con ser uno yo
Soy Jesucristo formado;
[Instantaneamente al suelo
Cae allí inmóvil y asustado.]
Pero dándome licencia
Segunda vez preguntado
Ejecutando el intento
Sin atender al milagro.
Siendo estos males futuros
Ya me contemplo amarrado
Y de los crueles sayones
Cual malhechor maltratado.
¡Ah, humana miseria y ciega!
No miréis tu ingrato daño;
Este es el madero verde
Que da el infecundo árbol.
Aquí el valeroso Pedro
Desenvainando el terciado
Con un impetuoso ánimo

seen may be avoided, since they are darts. Although all (in this world) be suffering, grief and insult, no one seeks to find surcease, pleasure or relief. Here was that night of sorrow, for even now my Father is praying in thought of my cross. I shall taste of the bitter cup. Here by coral streams mixed with the crystal drops of sweat the fragrant flowers are to be crimson carnations. This is the place where a deep sleep has befallen me; my beloved disciples are my guard. Here the evil Judas, a traitor, false, filled with avarice and guile, will hand me over to my enemies. Oh envy, viper, ugly and cunning, atrocious without repair, you will not cease to live until the world shall no longer exist. So, although I am but one, I am the Christ in human form. Instantly fear strikes him (the soldier) to the ground, but I, withholding my power, allow the question a second time and submit to arrest. These evils being yet to come, I already see myself bound and mistreated by cruel executioners as though I were an evil-doer. Oh mankind, wretched and blind, look not upon your ungrateful offense; this is the green timber which the barren tree furnishes (for the cross). Here the brave Peter unsheathing his sword with impetuous courage will cut off the ear of Malchus. Now I would leave the garden and by the brook of Kedron con-

Cortará la oreja a Malco.
Salir quiero ya del huerto
Y proseguir meditando
Por el arroyo Sedrón
La furia de los soldados.
Por aquí con irisión,
Escupido y blasfemado
De injurias y con tormentos
Seré de todos el blanco.
De la pesada cadena
Vengativos como airados
Unos me celebrarán
Y otros detendrán mis pasos;
Fuerte lance y que en el suelo
Me pondrán desapiadados
Y alzándome con violencia
A coces y a puntillones.

tinue meditating upon the rage of the soldiers. Here I shall be mocked of all, spit upon, insulted and tormented. Laden with the heavy chain, vindictive and angry ones will mock me and others will seek to detain my steps. A terrible moment! Cruelly they will place me on the ground, then raise me violently by kicks and blows.

Angel

Ánimo, niño Jesús;
Vamos prosiguiendo, vamos;
Viva el hombre y muéras tú,
Pues quisiste ser su hermano.

Angel

Courage, child Jesus! Let us continue, come; let man live and you die, since you wished to be his brother.

El Niño

Los estremos del amor
Antes que sin el caso
Se conocen vinculados
En la operación que operaron
El amante y los soldados.

The Child

The soldiers in executing their will upon the lover (Christ) but exemplify the extremes which love can encompass.

[*Cristo al*] *Primer Palacio*

Esta es la casa de Anás
Ante quien el caso,
Por ser suegro de Caifás
Primero será entregado.
Adulación, quien te abriga
Siempre andará tropezando
Sin tener tramito diéstro,
Del verdadero descanso,
Porque todo aquel que adula
Procura ser adulado;
Haber alivio ninguno
Fuera de mi puede darlo.

[*Christ at the*] *First Palace*

This is the house of Annas, before whom, as he is the father-in-law of Caiphas, the case will first be heard. Oh flattery! Whoever harbors you in his breast will always go stumbling along without ever taking the right step toward the true resting place, because he who flatters seeks to be flattered; no one outside of me can give peace.

[Cristo al] Segundo Palacio

Del Pontífice Caifás
Es este soberbio palacio
En donde de mi doctrina
Por él seré preguntado.
Como sacerdote al fin,
Aunque sacerdote malo
Profetizaron también
Que yo moriría atormentado.
Aquí el único sayón
Iracundo y denodado
Sin ver mi justa razón
Herirá mi rostro sacro.

[Christ at the] Second Palace

This palace belongs to the pontifex Caiphas, and here I will be questioned concerning my teaching. Finally as a priest, although an evil one, they have prophesied that I would die tortured. Here the only executioner, angered and insultingly, without seeing my just cause will wound my holy face.

[Cristo al] Tercer Palacio

Este es el palacio altivo
En que hoy habita Arquelas;
Vivirá Herodes por quien
También seré preguntado.
Con una púrpura manta
Rota por gusto y escarnio
Seré vuelto a la presencia
Del emperador romano.

[Christ at the] Third Palace

This is the palace in which today lives Arquelas, but in which Herod shall live, by whom I shall also be questioned. Clothed in a purple robe torn by the will of the crowd, I shall be returned to the Roman emperor.

[Cristo al] Cuarto y último palacio

Este es el palacio y casa
Del gobernador Pilatos
¡Ay dolor! ¡De qué rigor
Me está aquí amenazando!
Al tránsito de mi muerte
Cuando me están azotando
Tres veces he de llegar
En una columna atado.

[Christ at the] Fourth and Last Palace

This is the house and palace of the Governor Pilate. Oh sorrow! With what cruelty this place is threatening me! In the approaching hour of my death three times will I be bound to a column and be scourged.

Niño

Por fin, de aquí tomaré
Camino del matadero
Como está profetizado,
Sin mover ni abrir mis labios
El hombre se vino a ver
Que con la leña cargado

The Child

Finally, from here I shall take the road to the place of death as has been prophesied. Without opening my lips, I find myself laden with the cross, and the true Messiah

Sale el verdadero Mesaías
Por vuestro amor al calvario.
Ovejuela ya perdida
Metida en vicios tan malos
Sumergida en el abismo
Abrazada en tantos daños.
Hasta cuando, pecador,
Apacentáis mi rebaño;
Habéis de oír mis voces
Metido en vicios tan malos.
Mirá que ha de llegar tiempo
Que os acordáis de mi llanto
Y que me habéis de dar cuenta
Del más mínimo pecado.
Oíd, pecador ciego y torpe,
Astuto, atroz sin reparo,
Atended a la justicia
Que os está aquí amenazando.
Ya con esta enfermedad
Los bárbaros ya matando
Cautivos los inocentes
Tu pecado ellos pagando.
Mirá que soy buen pastor
Y conozco mi ganado,
Con un amén me llamáis
Y os recibiré en mis brazos.
¡O así como vengan todos
Misericordia a implorar!
Será tanta la epidemia
Y los perdonaré su agravio.

goes out, for love of you, to Calvary—a lost sheep surrounded by evils, submerged in the abyss, overtaken by many sorrows. How long, oh sinner, will you thus treat my flock? You shall hear my voice, although sunken in sin. The time will come when you will remember my sorrow and render an account of the smallest sin. Listen, oh sinner, blind and stupid, shrewd and wicked without amendment, see the justice that is threatening you. Possessed by this same infirmity, the barbarians are slaughtering innocent captives who are suffering for your sins. See that I am a good shepherd and know my sheep. With an "amen" you will call me and I will receive you in my arms. Oh may all come to seek pardon and mercy! The infirmity will be great and I will pardon them their offense.

Rico

¡Qué compostura de niño!
Llegáis con bien;
¿Qué se ofrece?

Rich Man

What a beautiful child! You are welcome. What do you wish?

Niño

A pediros, si merezco.
Por amor de Dios os pido
De necesidad forzado
Me concedáis un bocado;
Que en todo el día no he comido.

The Child

I come to ask alms of you if I am deserving. Forced by necessity, I beg you in God's name to give me a bite to eat, for I have tasted nothing in all this day.

Rico

Arragante sois, por cierto
Y pedís con gran descaro
Conociéndose bien claro
O estáis en la ley despierto.

Rich Man

Proud you are, in truth, and you beg with great impudence; that is clear, or you are well skilled in the law.

Niño

Señor, si satisfacción
De mí la queréis tomar
Bien me podréis preguntar
Lo que os parezca razón,
Porque si la variedad
De opiniones [fuere dada],
Si queréis ver [concertada]
Yo soy la suma verdad.

The Child

Sir, if you wish to take satisfaction of me, you may indeed ask me what may seem to you reasonable; for if among various opinions you wish the truth, I am the sacred truth.

Rico

La suma verdad es Dios
Pero vuestra tierna infancia,
Eso no es a la ley ignorancia,
[Ese] es un decir atroz;
¿Tenéis padres?

Rich Man

The perfect truth is God. For you who are not ignorant, though youthful, to speak as you speak is atrocious. Have you parents?

Niño

Sí señor, dos padres tengo;
Uno en el cielo y otro en el suelo,
Y hace tres días que los pierdo.

The Child

Yes, sir, I have two fathers, one in Heaven and another on earth, and I have been separated from my parents for three days.

Rico

Por ser criatura de Dios,
Gozáis del común privilegio
Universal de ser hijo suyo
Pero lo que intento es saber
Si vuestros padres vagos
Os dan tan malos ejemplos
Que en contra de nuestras leyes
Andáis vagante pidiendo.

Rich Man

By being one of God's creatures you enjoy the universal privilege of being His son, but I wish to know if your idle parents furnish you with such a bad example that you go about begging in violation of our laws.

Niño

Reporta, señor, tu ira
Si os enojáis como pienso;
Satisfacción os doy al punto
Y os dejaré satisfecho.
La causa de que en las leyes
Pusiera Dios el expreso
De que no hubiera mendigos
En el escogido pueblo
Puede dar a entender al rico
Que fuera de Dios dispensero
Ejecutando en elpobre
Transito y reportamiento.

The Child

Calm your anger, sir, if, as I think, you are angry; I shall satisfy you immediately and leave you entirely content. The fact that God put in the laws the express command that there should not be among the chosen people any beggars may give the rich man to understand that he is God's steward, obligated to show charity and kindness to the poor.

Rico

[Es clara tu pretensión]
Con que venís arguyendo
Muy medida al paladar
Con oscuros fundamentos.
Y si no, decidme [vos]
Vos prosiguiendo
[Siendo] el sumo poder
De Dios absoluto, os digo
Que este punto no toquemos.
De la potencia ordinaria
Os digo, que es caso necio
De privar a las criaturas
Los despóticos progresos
Que dió a la naturaleza
En el instante primero.

Rich Man

Your pretension is clear and you argue it with words that are very pleasant to the palate, though your premises are obscure. Whatever you say of human power, let us not speak of absolute power, which is an attribute of God alone. I tell you that it is foolish to deprive God's creatures[2] of powers and gifts originally bestowed by nature.

Niño

Bien está si no los priva;
A su pregunta os concedo.

The Child

It is well if God does not remove them; I grant your question.

Rico

Reconoceremos luego
Que lo que es ley natural
No destruye sus preceptos

Rich Man

This being granted, let us pursue the law to its sources, not excepting the maimed, the

[2] The rich people, the prerogatives of whom the *Rico* continues to justify.

Y siendo tan natural
Que la posada busquemos
Sin excepción de aquel que es
manco
Tullido, leproso o ciego,
Todos a un mismo "tenor",
Que razón encontraremos
De que trabaje el anciano
Para que coma el mancebo;
Y así muy mal persuadido estáis
Y vais muy lejos de eso
De dar plena inteligencia.
A lo que estás arguyendo
Y para que no lo ignores
En lo literal del texto
Que como Dios escogió
Por su agrado a nuestro pueblo
Hizo noble a sus criaturas
Y no quiso que pidiendo
Andemos de puerta en puerta
Cual si fueramos plebeyos.

halt, the leper or the blind from observation, all in the same manner. Thus shall we see why the old work that the young may eat. You then are ill-advised and your knowledge is far from complete. I shall reply to your argument and not leave you ignorant of the law. God in His own pleasure chose us to be His noble creatures and ordained that we should not go from door to door begging alms as if we were plebians.

Niño

Señor, que mata la letra;
Ningun fundamento entiendo.

The Child

Sir, the letter of the law kills; I understand no such principle.

Rico

¿Y qué me queréis decir?
Que esto que decís no niego.

Rich Man

And what do you wish to say? I do not deny what you say.

Niño

Para dar el resumen digo
Que el gran fundamento
En virtud que la limosna
Inclina el dador al cielo
Y como se ha de granjear
Si falta el merecimiento
Luego la proposición
Que hacéis, señor, lleva riesgo.

The Child

Summing up, I say that the law is founded on the fact that charity inclines the giver toward heaven provided he be worthy of heaven; otherwise, if merit be lacking, then your proposition, sir, is in danger of being a fallacy.

Rico

Trae el vino, Carrasco.

Rich Man

Bring the wine, Carrasco.

Carrasco

Aquí está, señor, y dos bachilleres.

Carrasco

Here it is, sir, and two bachelors.

Rico

Idos, bachilleres, de aquí
O desataremos los perros.

Rich Man

Leave here, bachelors, or we will set the dogs on you.

Carrasco

Todo el susto lo llevó
El mancebito por real y medio.

Carrasco

The young man had all his fright for a few cents.

Niño

De la tentación alarde
Hace este rico opulento;
Porque para el avariento
Siempre el pobre llega tarde.
Yo soy la causa primera
Mas por mi ciencia profunda
Dejo que obre la segunda
A lo que indignarse quiera.
Porque con mi poderío
Le dí al hombre libertad
Para elegir bien o mal
El don de libre albedrío.
Del mejor campeón es gala
Contar, a veces, el cuerpo
Vinculando en una fuga
De infinitos vencimientos.
¡O mundo! y cómo me pagas
Mis apreciables esfuerzos
Con que para corregirte
Vine de mi padre eterno.

The Child

This man rolling in wealth makes a boast of temptation, because for the rich man the poor man always comes too late. I am the first cause, but through my wisdom I allow the second to work its own will, because by my power I have given mankind the power to choose either good or evil, through the gift of free-will. It is satisfaction to the greatest champion, at times, to count a flight among his many victories.

Oh world! How ill you pay me for the great efforts with which I came from my Father to right you.

Rico

Vaya, que es mozo [travieso]
El mendigo, que cuando llegue
De los años a lo serio
No ha de haber ningún rabí
Que le matenga argumento.
Alza la mesa, Carrasco,
[Y venga conmigo Lelio.]

Rich Man

Come, this beggar is a cunning child, and when he comes to be of a serious age there will be no rabbi who can oppose him in an argument. Clear the table, Carrasco; come with me, Lelio.

Carrasco

Mis profecías se han cumplido;
Mi amo se portó grosero,
Pudo darle al mancebito
Lo que gastó en el jilguero.

Carrasco

My prophecies have been fulfilled; my master acted very meanly; he might have given him what he spent on the dog.

Letra

Gosabel regocijada,
Llena de impulso [y cariño]
Manda prevenir las viandas
Para sustentar al niño.

Chorus

Gosabel rejoicing, full of good will and charity, orders the viands prepared to sustain the child.

Gosabel

Rosaura, no sé que impulso
Espiritual me ha venido
Tan intenso que suspende
Mis potencias y sentidos
Y que estas célebres pascuas
Superabundantes han sido
Que lo que no me penetra
No puede el labio decirlo.
Y hoy con especialidad
Y con los dorados hilos
Y resplandores del día
Nuevas alegrías consigo.
Rosaura, prevén la mesa.

Gosabel

Rosaura, I do not know what spiritual impulse has come over me, so intense that it overwhelms my strength and senses; these famous feast days have been too much. What I do not understand my lips can not utter, and today especially with the golden rays and splendor of the day I have felt a new joy. Rosaura, set the table.

Niño

Lo primero, que ha tres diás
A mis padres he perdido;
Lo segundo, que en todo hoy
Ningún sustento he tenido;

The Child

First, it has been three days since I have lost my father and mother; second, I have had no food in all this day; third,

Lo tercero, qué dolor
Que llegué a casa de un rico
A tiempos que con grandeza
Comiéndose a su beneficio
Y conmigo anduvo escaso.
Cuando en lo demás propicio;
Negóme al fin un bocado,
Habiéndome entretenido
Con preguntas y respuestas
Muy a lo lejos de sus oídos
Porque la verdad, señora,
[Con un desnudo sentido]
Matan a aquel que pudiera
Servirles del lumitivo.

what pain I felt when I came to the house of a rich man at the time when he was in all his grandeur eating for his own satisfaction. He behaved toward me miserly, though in other respects he was propitious; he denied me a bite after having diverted me with questions and answers far from his own understanding, because in truth, madam, with a brutal phrase they kill the one that would lead them to light.

Gosabel

Siéntate y sosiega, infante,
Y no extrañes lo omitido
Que mi espírtu inflamó
Con singulares auxilios.

Gosabel

Be seated and rest, child, and do not wonder at anything that may be lacking, for today my spirit has burned with singular encouragement.

Niño

¡Ah, señora! yo aseguro
Por lo que mi madre me ama
Que han de pasar tres días
Que no la veo la cara.

The Child

Ah, madam, I assure you by all the love that my mother bears me that three days are to pass in which I do not see her face.

Gosabel

Come, niño de mi vida,
Come y no derrames perlas
Que yo buscaré a tus padres
Breve en toda la Judea.
Come, señor, y desecha
Los cuidados que te asaltan,
Que por la imaginación
Que dices que te acompaña
Es muy poco lo que comes
Y mucho lo que te extraña.

Gosabel

Eat, child of my life, eat and let not those pearls continue rolling down your cheeks; I will shortly search for your parents in all Judea. Eat, sir; throw off those cares that assail you, for on account of that image which you say never leaves you, you are eating very little and wondering a great deal.

Niño

Estas ternuras me sacan
Las lágrimas de los ojos
Anulando a la garganta.

The Child

This tenderness of yours brings tears to my eyes and chokes my throat.

Gosabel

Así lo creo yo;
Gozara de dicha tanta
De ser tu madre, señor,
Más que a mi vida te amara.

Gosabel

So I think. What happiness would I enjoy were I your mother, sir; I would love you more than life.

Niño

Oh señora, que mi madre
Sin que yo pondere nada
Me quiere y me idolatra;
Ya voy, señora, a poner
Los afectos que os embargan
En servir y amar a Dios,
Como que es primera causa.
Por tan raros beneficios
Os doy, Gosabel, las gracias,
Asegurando será
A satisfacción la paga.
Si aquí llegase mi madre
Procuréis consolarla
Diciendo que voy al templo
A negocios de importancia.

The Child

Ah, madam, my mother—and I do not need to exaggerate—loves me and idolizes me; I am now going, madam, to lay down those causes which prevent you from serving and loving God, since that is the first consideration. For such rare kindness, Gosabel, I give you thanks, assuring you that the reward will be your satisfaction. If my mother should come this way, try to comfort her and tell her that I am going to the temple on matters of importance.

Gosabel

Lo que no puedo explicar
Lo que no consigo y distingo
Lo natural se dice
Pero en lo que es divino
El discurso que tú haces
Es el común en que vivimos.
De los que de un saber
Hacen ruidosos designios
Las alegrías naturales
Y espirituales alivios
En dos opuestos extremos

Gosabel

What I can not explain or specify, you have spoken. As to divinity, your words are the ones by which we live. Regardless of those who make a noisy show of wisdom, natural joys and spiritual alleviation proceed from opposites: from much to nothing and from nothing to the infinite. We are nothingness; goodness is eter-

Tienen estos distintivos:
Lo que va de mucho a nada
Y de lo nada a infinito.
Porque nuestra nada es suma
Y eterno aquel beneficio
Y así es el objeto
En grado superlativo
Sobrenatural se alcanza
Nuestra dureza su estilo
Y tan solamente siente
El alma como es resquicio
En un embrazo amoroso
Me parece de ser [decisivo).
¿Me has entendido, Rosaura?

nal. Thus is our aim superlative. Our hardness realizes its own nature and only the soul feels the loving embrace. The matter appears to me evident. Have you understood me, Rosaura?

Rosaura

Ya, señora, te he entendido
Que puede ser este infante
Que para acá se encaminó
Entre las sombras de un humano
Tenga mucho de a divino.

Rosaura

I have understood you, madam. This child whose way led him here may underneath his human form conceal much that is divine.

Gosabel

Siento apartarme del niño
Desde luego que lo ví
Me constituí por su esclava.

Gosabel

I regret to leave the child; as soon as I saw him I became his slave.

Rosaura

Y yo pensé que la gloria
Se había mudado a esta sala.

Rosaura

And I thought that glory had taken its abode in this hall.

Laura

Con la vista alegra el niño,
Nada pondera Rosaura;
Dichosa la esclavitud
Que se vincula en su gracia.
Vamos, señora, que yo
Me había quedado elevada.

Laura

With his look the child brings happiness to one; Rosaura does not exaggerate; happy is the servitude linked with his grace. Come, madam; I was raised to the stars.

Gosabel

La doctrina celestial
Que me alumbra, su eficacia,
No se opone que redima
En Dios y por Dios con ansia;
Porque todo peregrino
En Dios y por Dios se alcanza
A no ser que de divino
Supuesto que no sea fianza
Porque solamente a ti
Se va [y no me estorba]
Por único hijo de Dios
Mi bendición te adora.
Ir con Dios
Toda mi atención me arrastra.
No vimos rara hermosura,
Rosaura, ven; vamos, Laura.

Gosabel

The efficacy of the celestial law that guides me is not opposed to redemption in and through God. Every earnest seeker attains something divine for himself, provided he trust not overmuch in himself, for man must seek you alone. My blessing hails you as the only Son of God. Seldom have we seen such rare beauty, Rosaura. Come, let us go, Laura.

Letra

¡O tristisima María!
Recibe mi voluntad;
De los que a tu soledad
Vienen a ser tu compañía.

Chorus

Oh sad Mary! Receive love from those who come to bear you company in your loneliness.

Virgen

En dolores y tristuras
Vivo, Jesús de mi vida,
Hasta no encontrar el Norte
A quien mis ansias suspiran.
Se esconden todos los medios
Que mis dudas esculpían
¿Qué mucho que entre estas faldas
Entre tinieblas metida.
De oscuridades cercada
Y de penas sumergida
Gritando mares al orbe
De aflicciones y agonías?
Aun el albedrío organizado
Se consume y aniquila
Pues que sintiera una madre
Aunque madre tan indigna
Con pleno conocimiento

Virgin

In grief and sorrow I shall live, oh Jesus of my life, until I attain that goal toward which my anxiety drives me. Means which my care would devise for finding you are denied me. What, then, does it matter that I, wandering in the shadows of these hills, surrounded by darkness, submerged in grief, should cry aloud to heaven in pain and agony? Even a mother's will, however firm, is consumed and melts away. A mother, however unworthy she may be, would grieve could she but know what I have lost. With

De la luz que traí perdida.
Con tu ayuda determino
En este tercero día
Ir al desierto a buscarte
A donde doble sería
A tu primo o precursor
Hayas hecho una visita,
Imitación a que hice yo
A Isabel mi prima.
Si allí no te encontrara,
Mi desvelo determina
Ir al portal de Belén
En busca de tus delicias.

your aid, on this the third day, I am determined to go to the desert to seek you. (Perchance) you have made a visit to your cousin or forerunner as I made to my cousin Elizabeth. If there I should not find you, my care determines me to seek at the gates of Bethlehem for your happiness.

Angel

Reina, señora, supuesto
Que Dios echó la cortina
A la vista perspicacia
Con que sumamente registra
Vuestra voluntad admirable
Toda la ciencia divina,
Consolaos con que es su gusto.
Admitido peregrino,
Buscando a aquel que buscáis
Desde el eterno escogido
Aunque a daros el consuelo
Necesario nos inclina
Vuestro llanto, aquel precepto
Nuestras voluntades liga.
Ni en Belén ni en el desierto
Hallaréis vuestras fatigas.
De Jesús cuyo alto nombre
A venerar nos obliga
Desde el cielo hasta el infierno
A postrarnos de rodillas.

Angel

Queen, lady, granting that God drew the curtain before the piercing look with which your wonderful love seeks, console yourself with knowing that it is His will. Confessed pilgrim, seeking that one whom you seek, chosen from eternity, although your tears incline us to give you comfort, high command binds our will. Neither in Bethlehem nor in the desert will you find the object of your care—Jesus, whose holy name obliges us all, from Heaven to Hell, to worship and bend the knee.

Virgen

Soberanos para mí
Que para mi compañía
El que es todo poderoso
Dispuso por obra y [guía]
Me resigno como esclava
Pidiéndote me dirijas
A seguir tu voluntad

Virgin

Sovereign is he whom the Almighty ordained to be my guide. I resign myself as a slave, begging that you direct me to follow your will and renounce my own. My spouse went to the city, and it is fit-

Y a renuciar de la mía.
A la ciudad fué mi esposo
Es razón que yo le siga;
Si propio bien nos arrastra
Si la atención una misma.
Y así, piadosas matronas,
Madres, las que tenéis hijos
Si acaso los enemigos
Se los llevasen cautivos
Y que supiesen que entre ellos
Buscando común alivio
El sustento le negasen
El castigo fuera [inicuo]
Sintieran estos trabajos
Que padecen vuestros hijos,
Pues que sintiera una madre
Que a su niño trae perdido.
Con pleno conocimiento
De su amparo y de su alivio
Desaten mis tristes ojos
Con abundantes rocíos
Que en mi propio amor se
aniegan
Las penas de mis conflictos.
Arroyuelos infecundos
Que sedientos de agua miro
Arrimaos a mis dos mares
Y seréis cada uno hijo.
Tórtolas tristes, llorosas,
Acompañéis mis gemidos
Que vuestro logro yo tal
Me viene en común nacido.
Si acaso sabéis sentir,
Venid a mí, pajarillos
Al son de mis tristes quejas
Acompañen mis gemidos.
Cordero manso, si os roba
El lobo atroz, fementido,
Si la ausencia de la madre
Llora triste y desvalido;
Acompañadme y venid
Ya inocente corderito,
Supuesto que mi Jesús
En la ciudad se ha perdido.
¡Ay, qué dolor, qué tristeza!
Ambos, señor, ¡Que conflicto!
Y conociendo en el alma

ting that I follow him, since one treasure draws us both and a common care possesses us. And now, pious matrons, mothers yourselves, should wicked enemies take your sons captive and then should [these sons?] find among themselves my son working for their common deliverance, how ill it would become them to deny him sustenance. You would sorrow for the ills suffered by your sons; a mother can but grieve for a son who is lost.

With full knowledge of his refuge and ease my eyes loose an abundance of dewy tears; for the sorrows for my conflicts are submerged in my own love. Barren brooks thirsty for water, come to my two seas of tears and each will be a son of mine. Sad, weeping doves, accompany me in my sighs, that our grief may be common. Birds, if you know how to grieve to the sound of sad complaints, accompany me in groans. Gentle lamb, if the fierce and wicked wolf robs you, if you weep for the absence of your mother, sad and helpless, accompany me! Come, innocent lamb, since my Jesus has been lost in the city. Oh what pain, what sadness, both, Lord! What conflicts! In my soul I sacrifice. Son of my heart, if you dwell in Jerusalem, you will be going from door to door seeking lodging; some will give you shelter, nobly and freely. May you give them eternal reward, which you owe them. Others

En el alma sacrifico.
Hijo de mi corazón,
Si en Jerusalén habitas
Andarás de puerta en puerta
Buscando la posadería;
Unos te socorrerán
Con franqueza y bizarría;
Tú les des la eterna paga
Que les tienes merecida;
Otros con dolor grosero
Te negarán la comida.
Perdonarles es virtud
Suya es la pérdida.
Siendo el verdadero pan,
Pobrecito de mi vida
Por un pedazo andarás
Rasadas tus dos mejillas.
Aquí está, señor, tu madre
Vuelve a mí, que socorrida
Será tu necesidad
Y mis lágrimas concluídas.

will angrily deny you food; it is a virtue to pardon them, for theirs is the loss. Although you are the true bread, yet you will go with sunken cheeks seeking a morsel. Here is your mother. Lord, come back to me; then will your every need be satisfied and my tears ended.

[*Aqui van juntos, San José y la Virgen y los ángeles.*]

[*Here the Virgin, Saint Joseph, and the angels go together.*]

San José

Las mayores diligencias
Me causan mayores ansias
Cuando entre deudos y amigos
No hallo razón de importancia.

Saint Joseph

The greatest diligence causes me the greatest anxiety, since among relatives and friends I find no information of importance.

Virgen

Esposo y señor, la pena
Que me impide las palabras
Y el acento doloroso
Que quiere explicar el alma.

Virgin

Spouse and lord, grief and tears hold back the words that my heart wishes to utter.

San José

Casta paloma, en quien Dios
Mis finos afectos ama

Saint Joseph

Pure dove in whom God cherishes my pure love, let us

Lleguemos de puerta en puerta
Que en Dios pongo la esperanza.

go from door to door, for in God I place my trust.

Virgin

Matronas, decidme
¿Dónde hallaré a mi constancia,
A la lumbre de mis ojos
Que hace tres días que me falta?
Es blanco y colorado
Una azucena su cara,
Salpicada de claveles
En partes proporcionada.
El pelo rubio, los ojos
Son dos lumbreras tan claras
Que de él toma el claro sol
Todo su ser y sustancia,
Su boca un coral partido
Tan dulces son sus palabras
Que cuando las fabrica
El cielo y tierra abrasan.
Tan fino que así quedó
La perla y mano tirana,
El cuerpo y alma se quedan
Con los mismos que le agravian.
Su cuerpo es un pino de oro
Que así amenaza su planta
El habita en el imperio
Tiene su asiento y morada.
Tan franco que de su mesa
Esparce tantas migajas
Que mantiene a sus criaturas
Así buenas como malas;
Tan bueno que todo aquel
Que de corazón le llama
Abandonando los vicios
Les perdona y les regala.
Estas señas, pormenores
Brevemente dibujados
Tiene el tesoro que busco
Miren si es justa mi causa.

Virgin

Mothers, tell me where I shall find my hope, the light of my eyes, now for three days missing? He is fair and rosy; his face is like a lily smoothly touched with carnations. His hair is fair. His eyes are two burning flames, so bright that the burning sun takes from them its substance and being. His lips are of coral; so sweet are his words when he utters them that Heaven and earth are inflamed. Altogether lovely, his hands as pearl, his body and soul remain with those who offend him. His body is like the golden pine; where his foot rests, there he dwells; in the world he has his place and dwelling. So generous is he that from his table he scatters so many crumbs that he sustains his creatures, good as well as evil. So good is he that all who earnestly call upon him and leave their evil ways he pardons and rewards. This description briefly details the treasure I seek. See then if my cause is not just.

Gosabel

Esta señora sin duda
Según viene amensurada
Es la madre de aquel niño
Que hoy regocijó mi casa.

Gosabel

This woman, without doubt, from her appearance is the mother of that child who today rejoiced our house.

Virgen

Matronas, hoy hace tres días
Que ando buscando con ansia
A la lumbre de mis ojos
Que he perdido en estas pascuas.

Virgin

Matrons, this is the third day that I have been in search of the light of my eyes, which I have lost during this feast.

Gosabel

Dénnos las señas, señora,
Y espero que consolada
Habéis de salir de aquí
Según los sinos declaran.

Gosabel

Give us the description, madam, and, unless all signs fail, you will leave here comforted.

Virgen

Es un niño de doce años
Pimpollo de amina y grana;
Pelo y rostro de mi esposo,
Mírenle muy bien la cara.

Virgin

He is a child of twelve years, a rosebud tender and pomegranate-hued. He has the hair and face of my spouse; look well at his face.

Gosabel

De necesidad forzado
Hoy merendó en esta sala;
Dejándome con dulzura
De mi misma enajenada.
Díjome que se iba al templo
A negocios de importancia
Y allí lo hallarás, señora,
Con redención en el alma.

Gosabel

Forced by need, he lunched today in this hall, leaving me with such peace that I was entranced with joy. He told me that he was going to the temple on matters of importance; there you will find him with redemption in the soul.

Virgen

Como me habéis consolado
Tengáis consuelo en el alma.
Dios os guarde.

Virgin

In the same measure that you have comforted me, may you find peace in your heart. God keep you.

Gosabel

Dios os guie
Hasta hallar la prenda amada.

Gosabel

God guide you until you find your beloved treasure.

Letra

Disputando entre doctores
La venida del Mesaías
El que está profetizado
Nos sacará de porfías.

Chorus

Disputing with the doctors concerning the coming of the Messiah, he whose coming has been foretold will free us from contentions.

El Niño

[*En medio de doctores.*]
Atendiendo a lo tratado
Y que os concedo, venía
[A] proponer dificultades
En la liberal palestra.
Digo pues tengo [oídos]
(Qué relación incierta!)
Los tan claros testimonios
Que al mundo confuso deja[n].
La venida del Mesaías
Tiene dos inteligencias:
Una ahora y otra después,
Como probará la letra.
Los profetas dicen
Que su venida ha de ser cierta
Con poder y majestad
Según alegado queda.
Dice Osaías que será
Legislador a su Alteza
Que ha de librar a su pueblo
De la servidumbre adversa;
Y también en otra parte
Afirma la pluma mesma
Que vendrá con tal furor
Que hará temblar a la tierra.
David también asegura
Que a sus gentes hará guerra
Abrasándoles con fuego
Por su impureza y dureza.
El Eclesiástico dice
Que vendrá en aquella hora
Con la multitud de santos
Patriarcas y profetas,
Y todas las escrituras
Las encontraremos llenas
Si con reflexión miramos
Así en la ejecución primera.

The Child

[*Among the doctors.*]
With regard to the matter under discussion—and I concede it—I came to propose some difficulties in this open debate. I heard (what a false account!) the clear testimony and evidence concerning the coming of the Messiah has confused the world. His coming has two interpretations: one now and another later, as the Scriptures prove. The prophets say that His coming is sure, with power and majesty. Isaiah says that He will be the lawgiver of the Most High, that He is to free His people from their oppressive servitude. Also in another place the same pen affirms that He will come with fury and make the earth tremble. David also assures that He will make war on His people, burning them with fire on account of their impurity and hardness of heart. The Ecclesiastic says that He will come in that hour with a multitude of saints, patriarchs and prophets, and we find all of the Scriptures full (of the prophecies) if we search them carefully. Thus it will be in the first judgment but in the second and in the other happenings foretold

Pero en la ejecución segunda
Y las otras concurrencias
Que parecen encontradas
Aun con la misma certeza
Porque dice el mismo Isaías
Que ha de venir a la tierra
Y que de las virtudes . . . .
Y que su generación es inmensa
O los verá numerosos . . . .
El [guarismo] de la cuenta
Que de oprobios será llenado
Y llevarle como oveja al matadero
A oír la más infame querella.

there is the same certainty. Because Isaiah himself (says) that He is to come to the world . . . . His followers will be great in numbers . . . . that He will be overwhelmed with insults and that He will be led as a lamb to slaughter to hear the most shameful charge.

Jeremías nos afirma
Que sus contrarios le acechan
Para castigarle al fin
Y borrarle de la cuenta.
Daniel dijo que sería
De todo el pueblo la afrenta
Hollado como gusano
De humilde naturaleza.
Zacarías, que vendrá
Manso y sentado en una bestia
Y en fin otras profecías
Que le dan la mano a estas.
Pues ¿cómo será posible
Convenir a estas promesas
Si no creemos dos venidas
Con debida inteligencia?
Una a redimir al mundo
Y otra a recibir la cuenta;
Luego en la una ha de venir
Y ha de ser en la primera,
Humilde, manso y tratable
Sin ejecutar violencia
A triunfar de Lucifer
Destruyendo su soberbia
De lo eterno espiritual,
Y a edificar nueva iglesia;
Y esparciendo para el hombre
Las apreciables riquezas
De dones y virtudes y gracias
Para ir a la vida eterna.
Esto es la verdad infalible
Como la fe nos enseña

Jeremiah tells us that His enemies will seek Him in order to punish Him and to kill Him. Daniel said that He would be as an affront to all people, trampled under foot as a worm, of an humble nature. Zacharias said that He would come meek and seated upon an ass; and finally other prophecies join these to the same effect. Then, how can we make these prophecies agree unless we believe in two comings? Manifestly one (coming) is to redeem the world and the other to receive the reckoning. In one interpretation He is to come—His first coming—humble, meek and kind, without using violence, to triumph over Lucifer by destroying his pride and power, and to found a new church. Then he will distribute among men the esteemed gifts, virtues and graces in order that they may inherit eternal life. This is the infallible truth as faith teaches us, determined and forseen from all eternity. The divine spirit of God, a

Determinada y provista
De la eternidad excelsa.
El espíritu divino
De Dios, una cosa mesma
Anduvo de boca en boca
Y de profeta en profeta
Con que pruebo que es venido
El Mesaías que espera.
El patriarca Jacobo
Nos dejó fijas sus señas
De su venida y faltando
El cetro real y diademas
Además de esto la señas
De Daniel ya están completas;
Luego el Mesaías es venido
Y entre vosotros se ostenta;
Es apoyo competente
El expreso de mí que haga
De que en Belén es la patria
Que escogió su Providencia.
Y en Belén hace doce años
Que hicieron permanencia
A unos humildes pastores
Se les intimó la nueva
De que era venido al mundo,
Y largando sus aldeas
Los tres reyes vinieron
Alumbrados de una estrella;
Por cuya razón, Herodes
A ver si encontraba vuelto
El Mesías, degolló
Su pureza, su inocencia
Esto es público y notorio,
Y por tal inteligencia
Seguro y no necesito
Recomendación ni prueba.

thing sustantive, passed from mouth to mouth and from prophet to prophet, proves that the expected Messiah has come. The patriarch Jacob left us infallible signs of His coming, lacking royal scepter and diadem; besides these, the signs which Daniel foretold are fulfilled. Then the Messiah is come and is dwelling among us. It is convincing proof that, following the commandments, I make Bethlehem, which Providence chose for me, my birthplace. For twelve years (my parents) have resided there. The news that the Messiah had come to the world was told to humble shepherds; the three kings, leaving their countries, came guided by a star; wherefore Herod, to see if he could find the Messiah returned, beheaded one pure and innocent. This fact is notorious and for such information certainly I do not need recommendation nor proof.

Isaiah

De la cuestión alegada
Sobre las diversas letras
Ayer quedó la disputa
Por no diferir abierta
En todo cuanto el discurso
Dificultades no encuentra
De conceder y negar
Les queda la puerta abierta.

Isaiah

With regard to the stated question concerning the various readings, the debate was opened yesterday; you have an open door for discussion in all points that do not involve denial (of God). Not one genuine reason (for believing that

Ninguna razón, genuina
Ha de encontrar vuestra vuelta
Porque si venido al mundo
El Mesaías que se espera
Hemos de dar en el blanco
Apurando la materia.
(Profundo niño, tan tierno.)

the Messiah has come) will your reconsideration find, because if the Messiah has come to the world we should find the truth by so exhausting the evidence.

(A profound youth, so tender.)

David

Daniel dice que las tribus
Y naciones altaneras
Unidas le servirán
Y prestarán obediencia.
Luego en tanta autoridad
En tan superior potencia
¿Que razón podrá existir
Para que oculto estuviera?
Dice el Eclesiástico
En enérgicas elocuencias
Y Jeremías nos afirma
Que en una nube ligera
Ha de destruir la gentílica
 potencia.
Es dado y no concedido
El caso llegado fuera
La noticia divulgada
Sonar ya en toda la tierra
En lo profundo del abismo.

David

Daniel says that all peoples and proud nations will unite in serving Him and giving obedience. Then with so much power and authority, what reason can exist for Him to remain hidden? The Ecclesiastic says with fiery eloquence and Jeremiah also affirms that in a filmy cloud He will come to destroy the Gentiles' power. It is patent that if the time had come, the news would be spread over the earth, even to the bottom of the pit.

Jeremías

Es así porque David
Enérgicamente aserta
Que ha de reinar majestuoso
Alrededor de la tierra
De mar en mar
Y así es dada la consecuencia
Que estos mismos fundamentos
Arguyen por quienes condenan;
Porque ni en la de Judea
Ni en otras tribus se espera
La restauración del cetro
Que hoy el romano maneja.
En lo que pregunta enseña.

Jeremiah

As David energetically asserts that He is to reign supreme in all the earth from sea to sea, so it is. Thus the very arguments proving His coming deny his having come. For neither in Judea nor among other tribes is there a sign that the scepter wielded today by the Roman hand will be restored (to us).
Even his questions teach.

Daniel

Recomiendo los principios
Que precede la esperanza;
Nuestros dos restauradores
Moisés y Aaron nos presentan
Para [negar] la venida
O elegir larga materia
Cómo si la libertad
De entre las tribus viniera
O por vía de milagro
Como de Moisés se espera
O por armas como [a giro]
Acreditada sorpresa.
(Nos confunde en lo que dice.)

Daniel

I recommend the principles on which hope is based; our two restorers, Moses and Aaron, furnish us a basis for denying that Christ has come and grounds for discussing how He is to come, provided He come from among His own people. Two ways are open: First, His coming may be a miracle as Moses thought; or second, He may declare Himself to us by means of some feat of arms, a notable victory. (He confounds us with His argument.)

Zacarías

Que no es venido confirmo
Y la razón lo argumenta;
Dios es fiel en sus palabras
Como dice el Real Profeta
Que ha de librar a su pueblo
De la servidumbre adversa
Luego estando como estamos
En la inaudita bajeza
Y servidumbre gentil
Que no es venido se prueba.
(Alegra con su mirada.)

Zacharias

I confirm the belief that He is not come and reason supports it; God is faithful in His words, and the royal prophet says that He is to free His people from grievous slavery; since we are in vile servitude to a Gentile race, it is evident that He is not come.

(His glance rejoices one.)

[*Habla Isaias otra vez.*]

En verdad que estando en Roma
El Rey con plena potencia
Todo cuanto dice el niño
Me escribieron con certeza.
Yo soy testigo de vista
De la milagrosa influencia
De una fuente que dió aceite
Veinte y cuatro horas enteras.
(Cuanto dice habla con alma.)

[*Isaiah speaks again.*]

In truth, the king being in Rome with full power, all that the child says they wrote me exactly. I am an eye witness of the miraculous influence of the fountain which flowed oil for twenty-four hours.

(What he says he speaks from his heart.)

Habla David otra vez.

Y Ananías lo profetiza
Con la apelación debida
Estando en Roma me escriben
Que se presentó a los treinta
De persuadido en el templo
Un niño tan singular
Que del Mesías tenía señas.
Y a otra vista conviene
Por lo que Isaías nos afirma
Que ha de nacer de una Virgen
Sin daño de su pureza.
(Dios guarde cosa tan buena.)

David speaks again.

And Annanias announces Him with the title due Him. In Rome they write me that a child presented himself before the thirty so striking in manner that he bore signs of the Messiah.

And further study is fitting on account of what Isaiah says: that He is to be born of a virgin without endangering her purity.

(God keep anything so good.)

[*La Virgen habla con el niño.*]

¿Cómo lo habéis hecho así?
Que con diligencia vuestro padre
Y yo os buscamos llenos de dolor.

[*The Virgin speaks with the child.*]

Why have you done thus? Your father and I, full of sorrow, have searched for you with diligence.

Niño

Pues para qué me buscáis?
¿No sabes donde me encuentran
Los negocios de mi padre
Me entrego a mis diligencias.

The Child

Well, why have you sought me? Do you not know that where the business of my Father finds me I give myself to its exercise?

Virgen

Vuestro padre y yo os pedimos
Vuestra santa voluntad.

Virgin

Your father and I ask your Holy will.

Doctores, todos juntos

José, os damos las gracias
De que des tan buena cuenta
De tener un hijo honrado;
Certifico que asi sea

Doctors, all together

Joseph, we thank you that you give such good account of yourself by having so honorable a son; I certify to His vir-

Por ser el más docto Rabí
Que magistra las escuelas.

tue, for He is the most learned rabbi that ever taught in the schools.

Doctores, todos juntos

Doctors, all together

Gracias al niño que a todos
Nos sacó de conferencias.

Thanks to the child who delivered us all from conferences.

FOLK NAMES OF TEXAS CACTI[1]

By DAVID HALL

Since man first began to examine the world about him he has attached names to plants. In Texas these folk names are known to more people than the scientific names which the plants bear. Examination of the folk terminology applied to cacti shows that almost every variety has acquired a local name. Usually it has been derived from some characteristic of the plant that impressed the folk-mind. Names for the same variety differ with the locality; sometimes the same name has been given to different varieties in different parts of the state. But most of the names, such as "living rock" and "devil's pin-cushion," are apt comparisons between the plant and some object. The "living rock" cactus *(Ariocarpus fissuratus)* grows almost flush with the surface of the ground, usually among rocks which it greatly resembles. Growing in the Big Bend region, outwardly it appears more like a rock than a plant.

The name "devil's pincushion," or "devil's head" cactus, is suggestive of the plant's formidable appearance. It is known to the scientific world as *Homalocephala texensis,* but Mexicans call it *manca caballo,* which means "horse crippler." The *Echinocactus horizonthalonius* is also known as the "devil's head"; *biznaga,* "melon" cactus, and "niggerhead" cactus are some of the other West Texas local names applied to both varieties, between which the average person does not distinguish.

The "button" cactus *(Epithelantha micromeris)* easily resembles a thick, white button, and ranges in size from a dime to a dollar; it is one of the smallest of American cacti. The *peyote* cactus, or "mescal button" *(Lophophora williamsii),* which has been used by certain tribes of Indians in religious rites, is known for its alkaloid content and narcotic effect when chewed. It is not difficult to see why early settlers applied the name "dry whiskey"; the first Spaniards called it a "sacred

[1] The writer recognizes as an authority the work *Texas Cacti,* by Mrs. Roy W. Quillin, director of the Witte Museum of San Antonio. Many of the folk-names contained herein are mentioned by Mrs. Quillin. (See "Transactions of the Texas Academy of Science," Vol. XIV, 1930.)

mushroom," because of the use to which the Indians put it, and because when dried it resembled a dried mushroom. In the Big Bend today it is known as the "dumpling" cactus.

It is evident that the "hedgehog" cactus *(Hamatocactus setispinus)* drew its name from its long spines; because of the hooked nature of some of the spines it is also known as "fish-hook" cactus. The "barrel" cactus *(Ferocactus wislizeni)* which is sometimes also called "fish-hook" cactus, probably drew its name of "barrel" from the fact that the Indians scooped out the interior of the plant and used the outer shell as a vessel, as they would a gourd. Some people possibly also derived the name from the trait the plant has of storing up a quantity of water in its stem and roots. Again this variety is sometimes called "candy" cactus because slices of it are boiled and dipped in sugar or syrup to form a sweetmeat. It is also known as the "mule" cactus.

Both the *Ferocactus hamatacanthus* and the *F. unicinatus* are known as the "Turk's-head" cactus, presumably because of their fez-shaped growth.

The *Ancistrocactus scheeri* is called the "root" cactus; a peculiar feature of the plant is the large and fleshy roots.

The "nipple" cactus *(Coryphantha sulcata)* is so named because of the oblong, spine-tipped tubercles which grow in clusters to form the plant; the fruit is also nipple-shaped. *Neomammillaria hemisphaerica,* or the "hemisphere" cactus, draws its name from its circular shape. The Mexicans call it *pichilinga;* it is the "pincushion" of some localities. Another member of the same genus *(N. applanata)* bears a scarlet, edible fruit known as a "lady-finger," and is for that reason known locally as the "lady-finger" cactus. The *Echinocereus pentalophus* is called the "finger" cactus, but here reference is made to the slender stems rather than to the fruit.

N. multiceps is the "hairy" cactus; small, gray spines cover its surface and give to it a "fuzzy" appearance.

At least two varieties, *Echinocereus stramineus* and *E. enneacanthus,* are known in the parts of the state where they grow as the "strawberry" cactus; their fruit, readily edible, has a strawberry color and flavor. The Mexicans call both fruit and plant *pitahaya.* The names "cob" cactus and "banana" cactus are also applied to the last-named variety in reference to its cob-like, or banana-shaped, stems.

The *Echinocereus reichenbachii* has many names due to the wide extent of its growth. The name "rainbow" cactus indicates the varying color of its spines; "lace" cactus refers to the character and appearance of its harmless spines; "merry widow" cactus alludes to the pink blossom, which is said to be the shape of the "merry widow hat," once popular in the United States. *E. dasyacanthus, E. viridiflorus,* and *E. chloranthus* are known respectively as the yellow-, green-, and brown-flowered *pitahayas.* All of them are called "rainbow" cactus, "rock" cactus, and "silkies." Another of the same genus, the *E. triglochidiatus,* is the "claret-cup" cactus, widely known and collected for its red, goblet-shaped blooms.

The "triangle" cactus of South Texas *(Acanthocereus pentagonus)* is called the "night-blooming" cactus; it is one of two varieties known by the Mexicans as *órgano* because its upright-growing stems resemble the pipes of an organ.

The names "deer-horn" cactus and "chaparral" cactus (both of which are applied to *Penicereus greggii)* and "lead-pencil" cactus and "dahlia" cactus *(Wilcoxia poselgeri)* are suggestive of the shape, habitat, and flower of the plants.

One variety of cactus found extensively in the state is the *Opuntia lindheimeri.* It, and a number of others of the same genus, pass under the folk-names "prickly pear" and "flapjack" cactus. The fruit of some varieties is called "pear apple," *tuna,* or "Indian fig" and is edible. These varieties were known as "mission" cacti in the days of Spanish Texas. It is said that the coyotes, in order to eat the fruit, whip the spines from it with their tails.

Most striking in appearance of all the "pears" is the "cow-tongue" cactus, or *lengua de vaca (O. linguiformis),* which is native of only a limited area south of San Antonio. The name is derived from the peculiar shape of the joints of the plant. Another variety is known in folk-language as the "purple pear" *(O. macrocentra),* its leaves having a deep, purplish color especially during the winter months. The "blind pear" of the Big Bend *(O. rufida)* probably received its name from the fact that the tiny thorns easily shake off and are said to sometimes blind animals nosing about them.

The "devil" cactus *(O. schottii)*, though not a "prickly pear," has long spines and forms masses sometimes fifty feet in diameter. Mexicans refer to it as *clavete,* which means literally "small nail or spike."

The most extensively-found cactus in the state is the *tasajillo (O. leptocaulis)* or "little-stemmed" cactus. It is the "lead-pencil" cactus in some parts of the state. The most common arborescent variety *(O. imbricata)* passes under a number of names, signifying the connection the plant has had with man. It is the "candle" cactus, "tree" cactus, "devil's rope," "coyote prickly pear," "walking-cane" cactus, *cholla* (skull), and *velas de coyote* (or coyote's candles). Another variety, the *O. davisii,* has earned the names "jumping-jack" cactus, "devil catcher," and "bull dog" cactus by its willowy stems and tenacious, straw-covered spines.

Some names are used for a great number of varieties. "Rainbow" cactus, "prickly pear," and *pitahaya* have already been mentioned. "Pancake" cactus is the name applied to several flat varieties. "Beaver-tail" cactus is the name of some spineless varieties of the "pear." Some *opuntias* have their spines covered with straw envelopes, which, seen by moonlight, take a glistening sheen; they are called "ghost" cacti.

Corruptions of some of the names may be noted. In Spain a *biznaga* is a carrot-like plant which grows sprigs used for picking the teeth; in Texas the corrupted forms *viznega, bisnagre,* and *biznega,* used by Mexicans, apparently mean anything covered with spines.

These home-grown names attest one simple fact: the folk-mind is quick to grasp the distinguishing characteristic of a plant, and to draw a comparison between that characteristic and some object which the plant resembles. These names belong to the soil.

CATS AND THE OCCULT

By MARTHA EMMONS

"For thar's a thousand reasons that I won't take time to tell
Why I am bound to b'lieve a cat is back and forth from hell."[1]

That is a bad name to give the inoffensive-looking house pet. But I fear the evidence bears out the hazard. From all accounts, the cat holds occult communication in some way. Whether he goes to the very lowest pit, as suggested by these lines, may be left open for a while. But his bad name seems to be well-nigh universal. According to Newbell Niles Puckett, E. N. Fogel, and others, the cat has established for himself a black reputation among the primitive folk of Europe as well as of Africa. And certainly the colored folk in America have no word of good fellowship or praise for old Tom and Tabby. The teller of merry tales steps gingerly aside from the cat as a subject. Even Uncle Remus, with his kindly attitude towards all the "critters," avoids the cat. He has much to say of Brer Rabbit, Brer B'ar, Wolf and the others, even to "Ole Sis' Mink," who is known to have anti-social habits. But of the cat Uncle Remus says nothing or nearly that.

Rarely does this gentle, purring fireside companion enter into the songs of the colored folk. In Talley's collection there is a four-line stanza about a cat and a fiddle.[2] In some of the jig-songs, the word "cat" appears as a nonsense syllable.[3] But in neither song nor story does this animal move in the jocund company of his fellows. When his name is mentioned, it is with mysterious or even sinister significance.

If the cat has few friends, the explanation is not far to seek. We must all acknowledge that he has some embarrassing habits. He eats his own children up. He sucks the breath out of the baby, right in the home where he is a trusted member. He prowls into any room where lies a corpse, and—worse yet—

[1] McNeill, John Charles, *Lyrics from Cotton Land*, p. 140. Stone and Barringer Company, Charlotte, N. C., 1907.

[2] Talley, Thomas W., *Negro Folk Rhymes*, p. 226. The Macmillan Company, New York, 1922.

[3] *Ibidem*, p. 9.

devours the corpse! He is far from amiable in appearance when he bows his back, flashes fire from his slit-like eyes, and spits. Nor is his smirking smile likely to be born of innocence.

The intimate relation of a cat with the supernatural makes him an omen of luck, sometimes ill, sometimes good. One may well dread having his path crossed by a black cat. Some say that if it crosses from left to right it is a good sign; while others reverse the direction, for luck. There has been much discussion over the question. But not long ago the straight of it was given to a friend of mine, in this way: "Ef'n a black cat wuz to cross from de lef'-han' side o' de road, hit tain' no bad sign; but I tell you, Mistuh Cholley, dey don' none ob 'em nevah cross dataway."

The luck that may possibly follow the keeping of a cat about the place all depends upon whether that cat is a witch, and if a witch, whether a good one. But if a cat comes to the house of its own accord, and "takes up" there, then it will bring good luck—unless it be a black one. The black cat seems to be an unwelcome guest everywhere. Rosanna, an industrious, happy colored woman in Waco, when questioned, side-stepped the issue in this way: "Hon, I don' b'lieve none o' that stuff 'bout witches; but I ain' gonna have no black aroun' me, 'cause I'se so black myself; an' devilish as I is, when me an' that cat would git to runnin' aroun' heah, you couldn' tell which un wuz me an' which wuz de cat."

That cats of any color are closely associated with witchcraft is too well attested to by reliable witnesses to be doubted. The black cat especially is a prime guise for a witch. A tale widely prevalent among Negroes identifies a beautiful woman in the form of a vicious cat. Many variants of this tale may be found. I have my version directly from Africa, by way of Annie May Zollicoffer, who retells it after her African father.[4]

According to Annie May, a certain man owned a gin—a feature added to the story, no doubt, in America. He could not keep a book-keeper. Every young man whom he employed would be speedily despatched, apparently by a witch.

[4] Annie May is a middle-aged Negro woman, of the old "darkey" type, living in East Waco. She has no apparent moral convictions, but has plenty of superstition.

At last, when the gin-owner found still another young bookkeeper stabbed and killed one morning, he decided he would take the job himself and find out about all this mischief. That night a beautiful white cat entered the office and crept stealthily toward him, as if to kill him. But the man was too quick for her. He turned and "stobbed 'er in de breas' an' cut 'er haid plum off." When he reached his home he found his wife lying covered up in bed, in a pool of blood, with a gaping wound in her breast, and her head severed from her body. Then he knew, of course, that it was his wife who had caused all the "devilment," and was happy to be rid of her.

The most popular variant of this story concerns a haunted house where no traveler ever spent a night and lived to tell the story, until once a wizard from the north stayed there. At midnight a black cat with two white paws came in and tried to kill him. He cut off its forefeet and put them in his handkerchief. The next morning after having breakfasted alone with the owner of the house, he asked to see the wife. He found her lying in her bed with both hands cut off at the wrists, and gone. When he looked in his handkerchief , lo, he held a woman's dead hands; and on the finger of the left hand was her wedding ring.

Cat-witches may be nearer to us than we think. Annie May tells of one who lives right here in Waco—a "white 'oman" who was for a time the employer of Annie May's daughter, Missouri. This woman soon proved herself to be a witch by periodically turning into a big black cat, "evah time she'd git mad at 'er husban'." This went on until Missouri's patience reached the snapping-point. "One day she come out whuh mah daughtah wuz a-washin'. She come whinin' aroun', an' wroppin' aroun' 'er laigs. Mah daughtah she up with a bucketful o' bilin' soapsuds outn de pot, an' she say, 'Looka heah, you come foolin' 'roun' out heah, I'll scal' you wid dish yer bilin' suds.'

"She quit 'er after dat. She say she ain' gonna wuck foh no witch, not when she know it. But, shucks, they's lots of 'em ovah theah that's witches. Folks jes' don't know it."

But the witch who interchanges her human form with the body of a black cat is playing with dynamite. As in conjuration, the black cat is a dangerous tool. It is understood that if one conjures by means of a black cat, he is literally "signing up wid de debbil."[5] No better off is the witch who goes in cahoots with the black cat. Annie May professes to have the power of a witch herself; she can, she says, take on almost any form. But she scorns the idea of a cat, saying, "You'd jes' as well be the Ole Nick hisself as to be a cat."

If a cat is associated with witches, he is on still more intimate terms with "ha'nts." And why should he not be? With all his nine lives—certainly he has a nine-to-one chance at haunting. It is known that the ghosts of good people, who die satisfied, do not come back; or if they do, they do not appear in animal or grotesque form. They come, if at all, for a definite purpose and go quietly about their business. But the mischievous ghosts—those who just go a-ha'ntin' for the fun of it, or to be up to mischief—these are of people who did not die satisfied. They are really "ha'nts." They assume a variety of forms, with the cat heading the list. Such "ha'nts" love to play pranks and to frighten innocent people. Especially do they delight in deserted houses. Many are the stories of "ha'nts" who as cats strike consternation to the heart of a tired traveler, just when he thinks he has found a quiet haven in a vacant house.

The indications are that cats, dead or alive, are up to all kinds of bad tricks. About the most decent use to which a cat ever puts his occult knowledge is to give warning. This story comes from the real experience of a colored man now living near Douglass, Texas. His miraculous warning was pictured to us in almost these exact words.[6]

Ford Wade's Dissertation

"Well, Missus, hit wuz dis away. I ain't been livin' lak de Lawd wan' me to, an' He knowed all about it. I got bad sick

[5] Puckett, Newbell Niles, *Folk Beliefs of the Southern Negro*, p. 257. The University of North Carolina Press, Chapel Hill, N. C., 1926.

[6] I am indebted to Miss Zillah Baker, of Nacogdoches, for this dissertation from Ford Wade, who was employed on her father's farm. She kept him bringing wood and warming before the fireplace long enough one morning to extract his story.

an' wuz in de baid a long time, an' de Lawd, He thought I wuz gwine die, Miss; so He know I'd bettah change mah way o' livin' 'fo' I cross dat rivah. I'd been in de baid so long I couldn' walk nary step. But one day I seen de biggest, blackest cat I evah seen come a-tearin' th'ough dat do'. He jump on dat baid an' grab me by de neck, a-chokin' me to death. Hm-m-m! I c'n jes' see 'im now! I sho' thought de debbil had me. Snakes bigger'n mah fist was a-crawlin' all ovah me. I jump out o' dat baid an' run down de road (an' 'fo' dat I couldn' walk a step) a-prayin' to de good Lawd to take away mah burden. I knowed, do', why de Lawd wuz a-doin' it, an' I promised evahthing de Lawd could ast.

"I went back to de house an' fell on my knees ag'in an' went to prayin' some mo'. I didn' eat nothin' foh three days, an' I prayed all de time. O, Lady, dey ain' nobody know what I done gone th'ough wid dem days.

"But finely de Lawd He tuck compassion on me, an' He rolled away de stone f'om de sepulchre o' my stony hea't, an' I ris' up, wid healin' in mah wings, a-singin' an' a-shoutin' de praises o' de Lawd God ob Hosts. An' evah sence den I been a-livin' foh de Lawd, an' I ain' nevah gonna forgit 'im no mo'. No, dat I ain'."

Score one for some constructive work of a cat. But woe to one so warned who heeds not.

The Deserted Village[7]

"Dey's a nigguh village in West Texas dat now's got only 'bout three families in it. Dey used to be about two hun'ud cullud families dah. But one time a ghos' in de shape ob a cat come dah, an' it had two haids an' eight laigs. He come to evahbody's house all time. Craps wuz fine out dah den; folks 'ud make two an' three bales o' cotton to a' acre: De ghos' would go into de houses o' de folks an' dey'd feed 'im. 'N'en dey'd tell 'im when dey wanted it to rain, an' hit 'ud rain.

"One day a nigguh gal cotch a little dove an' put it in a cage.

[7] Mr. Paul Stephens, of Nacogdoches, had this story from a Negro who worked for his family.

De ghos' come dat night an' say, 'Ef'n you don't turn dat fowl out, you'll die on the third day.' "

"Well, she didn' tu'n it out, an' sho' 'nough, on the third day she died, an' after de fune'al was ovah, dat ghos' come an' stood on her grave. Yas, sah, hit suttinly done dat thing, 'cause my pa he wuz dah, an' he seen it!

"Den all dem cullud folks dey 'cided to kill de ghos'. Dey got after it wid dawgs, runs, and hosses. De dawgs tracked it ahead an' caught it; but 'fo' de folks got to it, de dawgs had done tu'n' it aloose. Hit nevah did come back no mo'. But de nex' day, all de craps wuz et up by ants, an' in a yeah's time dey wuzn't but three fam'lies livin' dah, an' dey'us all white 'uns, an' livin' on poultry fahms."

One never knows when the most sociable of cats may turn out to be a witch or "ha'nt," or to have evil concourse with the occult world. Elmira tells of an old couple with whom a big old yellow cat "took up." They were glad to have her, and treated her kindly. All went well until one day—

The Black Cats' Message

"The ole man was a wood-cutter. One evenin' as he was comin' home from his work, he saw a passel o' black cats out in the road. He looked to see what they was doin', an' theah was nine black cats totin' a little dead cat on a stretcher. He thought, 'Well, I never heard o' sich a thing as this: nine black cats totin' a little dead cat on a stretcher.'

"Jes' then one o' them cats called out to the ole man an' says, 'Say, Mistuh, please tell Aunt Kan that Polly Grundy's daid.'

"The ole man nevah answered 'em; he jes' walked on a little peahtah; but he thought, 'Um-m-m! If this ain't the beatin'est thing, them cats a-tellin' me to tell Aunt Kan that Polly Grundy's daid.' Who is Aunt Kan, I wonder; an' who is Polly Grundy?

"Well, he jes' walked on, an' presen'y one of 'em hollered ag'in, an' say, 'Say, ole man, please tell Aunt Kan Polly Grundy's daid.'

"He jes' walked on ag'in, gittin' a little faster all the time;

an' presen'y all of 'em squall out: 'Hey there, ole man, please suh, tell Aunt Kan Polly Grundy's daid.'

"Then the ole man he broke into a run, an' he nevah stopped till he got to his house. He thought he wouldn' tell his ole 'oman nothin' about it. But that night he was settin' befo' de fiah eatin' his suppah—ole folks lots o' times eats dey suppah befo' de fiah—an' while his wife was a-settin' it foh 'im, he say, 'Well, Ole 'Oman, I guess I'll tell you some'n' dat I didn' think I would tell you.'

"When he say that, the ole yellow cat got up f'om de corner wheres she'us a-layin', an' come ovah an' set down right by his chaiah, a-lookin' up at 'im.

"His ole 'oman say, 'Well, what is it, Ole Man? I knowed they'uz some'n' on yo' min' when you come in at dat do'.'

"He say, 'Well, when I 'uz comin' in from de woods dis evenin', walkin' down de road, right theah in de road I seen a whole passel o' black cats. When I went ovah an' looked, theah was nine black cats a-totin' a little daid cat on a stretcher; an' them cats squall out to me three diffunt times an' tell me to tell Aunt Kan that Polly Grundy's daid.'

"When he say that, ole yellow cat jumped up an' say, 'Is she? B'God, I mus' go to the buryin'! An' out that do' she flew, an' she ain' nevah come back yit!' "

OLD-TIME NEGRO PROVERBS

By J. MASON BREWER

One morning when Uncle Israel, the old milk peddler, came to Aunt Patty's cabin, he was surprised to hear Hebe ask, "Uncle Israel, Mammy says huccom' de milk wattery in de mawnin'."

"Tell yo' mammy," replied Uncle Israel, "dat's de bes' sort o' milk. Dat's de dew on it. De cows been layin' in de dew."

"An' she tol' me to ax yuh,' continued Hebe, "whut make de milk so blue."

"Yuh ax yo' mammy," replied Uncle Israel, "whut make she so black."

Uncle Israel proved himself equal to the emergency. It takes a great deal of audacity indeed to pronounce upon the origin and age of proverbs, but, encouraged by Uncle Israel's example, I shall in listing and explaining the meaning of a number that I have collected attempt to fix the period and circumstances of their origin. For the most part those here given have been taken from the speech of ex-slaves and elderly Negroes living in central Texas, if not on farms then with a rural background. However, such proverbs are to be heard in the homes of the best educated Negroes of the country as well as in those of the lowliest.

While the pithiest and most savory proverbs seem to have come directly out of the Negro's own wisdom as well as environment, some of them are but transmutations of older expressions into the language and experience of the Negro. Thus, as the Bible has it, "Whatsoever a man soweth, that shall he also reap." As the old-time Negro has it, *Yuh kin sow in mah fiel' ef yuh wants to, but when hit comes, hit'll be in your'n an' yuh won't know how it got dere.*

As a slave, so far as his life was reflected in song and proverb, the Negro's primary interest seems to have been in God and religion. The much exploited "Work Songs" and the proverbs dealing with work probably developed during and after Reconstruction, at a time when the master no longer provided food, when the Negro had to rustle for himself and family and could not logically continue to pray God to take him "home" and free him from slavery.

Ol' Massa take keer o' himself, but de niggah got to go ter God conveys about the same idea as that in a saying once current among vigorous frontiersmen: "Lord, take care of the poor and us rich devils will look out after ourselves."

God and Freedom were with many slaves synonymous. *Yuh mought as well die wid de chills ez wid de fever* not only goes back to a common plantation malady but was interpreted for me as meaning that "you might as well get killed trying to escape as to remain a slave and die in slavery."

De quickah death, de quickah heaben, I heard an old woman say, and then she sang a song to enforce the idea of the proverb:

Oh Freedom, Oh Freedom,
Befoh Ah'd be uh slave
Ah'd be buried en mah grave
An' go home tuh mah Jesus an' be saved.

Much of the slave's time was spent in trying to find ways and means of escape. *Don' crow tel yuh git out o' de woods; dey mought be uh beah behin' de las' tree* meant "Don't be careless about talking to people you see, until you get to the Underground Railway. You might get caught and returned to your owner."

Don' say no mo' wid yo' mouf dan yo' back kin stan' is an admonition to slaves to speak briefly and seldom, not only to the master but to other slaves. Frequently the slaves would discuss the possibilities of escape among themselves, and be overheard by the overseer, some tattling slave, or the master himself; then his back paid for what his mouth had said.

You got eyes to see and wisdom not to see was an injunction to the slaves not to tell on each other about the neglect of duty, some clandestine visit to a neighboring plantation, the theft of a chicken or a pig, or any other misdemeanor.

Evah bell yuh heah ain't uh dinnah bell carries with it the idea that there was also a "rising bell" in the morning which called the slaves up for the day's work.

Of my entire collection I assign the most originality to a proverb given me by Aunt Milly Hicks, of Austin: *De one dat drap de crutch de bes' gits de mos' biscuits.* "What do you mean," I asked, "by drappin' de crutch?" "Dat means," explained Aunt Milly, "de one dat curt'sy de bes'." "Oh," I said, "you mean the one that could bow the most polite?" "Yas, suh, yas, suh, dat's hit," answered Aunt Milly, "an' Ah allus got de biscuits." This proverb carries with it more than Aunt Milly could express. It expresses the idea that the most polite slave got the easiest job on the plantation.

Don't let no chickens die in yo' han' implies the proverbial connection of the Negro with chickens. The idea is that when the dead chicken is on the ground instead of in his hand evidence against the darkey who has killed it is less incriminating.

As inevitable as chickens is cotton. The obvious meaning of *Dirt show up de quickes' on de cleanes' cotton* is that a bad deed shows up more distinctly on a person of good character than on a person of already bad repute.

Distant stovewood am good stovewood meant that the biggest trees don't grow on the edge of the woods and that if a man wanted big back logs for his fireplace, he would have to go to extra trouble to get them.

Muddy roads call de mile-post a liah belongs in the category of work proverbs.

Whut yuh don' hab in yo' haid yuh got ter hab in yo' feet. "Dat me'ns lak dis," said Uncle George McKay. "Lak ef yuh goes to de sto' fer some grub an' yuh fergits ter git it all, den yo' feet hab ter take yuh back anudder time fer whut yuh didn' git de fus' trip."

Dere's uh fambly coolness twixt de mule an' de singletree does not so much say that a mule sometimes kicks the singletree to which his traces are hooked as that two factors bound together, as man and wife, do not always work in harmony.

Although the ex-slave was grateful to God for his freedom and "God's chillun" were not supposed to dance, among the first of the freedman's free acts was a surrender to the rhythmic nature inherited from his African ancestors. He had, as a slave, developed into an excellent clog and tap dancer but had not been free to cultivate the social dance. The "platform dance" and the "cakewalk" came with Emancipation and the freedman revelled as much in dance and song as he had formerly revelled in church worship. Certain proverbs seem to date from this era of dancing and the freer courtship that came with it.

Don' take no mo' tuh yo' heaht dan yuh kin kick offen yo' heels meant, "Don't worry so much about jilts in love that you can't go to a dance and dance your troubles away."

Evahbody say "goodnight" ain't gone home may have evolved as a result of this social freedom enjoyed by the freed slave, especially by courting couples.

The philosophy of Negro gossip is summed up in the proverb, *Two niggahs 'll draw fo' niggahs an' fo' niggahs draw eight.*

To the Negro religion is always Alpha and Omega. I began this paper with slave proverbs on God and religion. I shall end with a proverb connected with religion and possibly of Reconstruction days: *Stah won' shoot fer de sinnah.* I have been told that when during Reconstruction Negroes attended a revival or a campmeeting and became converted, they would, if in doubt as to the authenticity of the conversion, ask, on the way home from the service, the Lord to "shoot" them a star. If then the convert saw a shooting star, it was a sign that he was really converted; but if he did not see a star shoot, there was still something lacking to his conversion, he had not yet been "born again," and he was still a sinner. Now some people claim that if a person keeps his gaze on one certain part of the sky for fifteen minutes, he will see a star fall and that, hence, there is nothing miraculous about the matter. Indeed, it is not likely that the gaze of man has anything to do with the falling or not falling of stars. The Negro, however, had unwavering faith in the belief and actually governed his decisions concerning conversion on the star sign. I recall hearing of only one instance in which a Negro who had asked for a shooting star failed to be convinced, when he saw it, that he had been born again and "washed in the blood of the Lamb."

A rousing revival was being conducted in Bell County, soon after the close of "the War," and finally Uncle Seth, who had not yet professed religion, was persuaded by his wife and children, members of the church, to attend the meetings. Before the services were over he had gone to the mourners' bench and professed religion. That night on the road home, however, his faith began to weaken. Knowing well the star test, Uncle Seth decided to try it out.

"Gawd," said Uncle Seth, "shoot me uh stah." In a few minutes he saw a star shoot across that part of the sky where he had his gaze directed. Not satisfied with this, however, when about halfway home, he repeated again, "Gawd, shoot me anudder stah." In a few minutes he saw another star shoot. This was not yet sufficient to get up Uncle Seth's faith; so when he was almost home, he said, "Gawd, looks lak hit's kinda hard fo' me to get up mah faith. Ah tells Yuh what Yuh do. Shoot me de moon." "The moon!" replied God. "I wouldn't shoot yuh de moon fer all de niggers in Texas."

Crude sayings of a crude people, humble, optimistic, good-humored. They have not all been collected.

Dey's jes' ez good uh fish in de creek ez evah been caught;
Dey's jes' ez good uh timber in de woods ez evah been bought.

NINETEENTH ANNUAL MEETING OF THE TEXAS FOLK-LORE SOCIETY, 1933

The Society met this year in Waco, on the campus of Baylor University, Friday and Saturday, April 21 and 22. There were four sessions. Owing to the death of John K. Strecker, president, during the year, Martha Emmons, long an active member of the Society and a resident of Waco, took the responsibility of getting the program up, and she presided. The programs follow.

FRIDAY AFTERNOON, APRIL 21

The Psychology of Folklore, Rabbi Wolff Macht, Waco.

Tales Wet and Dry, H. B. Parks, San Antonio.

Archaeological Treasures of Monte Albán, Professor Clyde C. Glascock, The University of Texas, Austin.

Tales About Early Mission History and the Indians, Elma Heard, Lufkin.

Folklore Contributions from West Texas:

1. *Witching for Water with the Bible.*
2. *Folk-Names of Texas Cacti.*

—David Hall, Brady.

FRIDAY AFTERNOON, APRIL 21

Memorial Hour for John K. Strecker, Deceased President of the Texas Folklore Society. At this time the Texas Academy of Science also gave public honorable mention of a bound volume of Mr. Strecker's contributions to science.

Folk-songs, by the South Junior Harmonica Band, Waco.

The Lore of Bees, Dr. Don O. Baird, Sam Houston State Teachers' College, Huntsville.

Excursions After Outlaws, Frost Woodhull, San Antonio.

How to Become a Member of the Texas Folklore Society, Dr. L. W. Payne, Jr., The University of Texas, Austin.

SATURDAY AFTERNOON, APRIL 22

Business session.

Cats and the Occult, Martha Emmons, Waco.

Old-Time Negro Proverbs, J. Mason Brewer, Samuel Huston College, Austin.

Jack Potter, Fighting Parson, J. Marvin Hunter, Bandera.

Musical number featuring Negro songs of Dave Gurley, by Baylor Choral Club, under the direction of Mrs. Allie Coleman Pierce.

Tall Yarns from the East Texas Cattle Country, Mrs. Ruth Garrison Francis, Beaumont.

Anecdotes of Historical East Texas Characters, Rev. George Crocket, Nacogdoches.

SATURDAY EVENING, APRIL 22

Subscription Dinner at the Raleigh Hotel, followed by:

Among My People, Jovita Gonzáles, Saint Mary's Hall, San Antonio.

Negro Spirituals, The Paul Quinn Octet, Waco.

Sing-song of Cowboy, Negro, and Other Folk Songs.

At the business session officers for 1933–34 were elected as follows: President, Frost Woodhull, San Antonio. Vice-Presidents, Martha Emmons, Waco; Newton Gaines, Fort Worth; Mrs. J. B. Kendrick, Gatesville. Councillors, M. L. Crimmins, San Antonio; L. W. Payne, Jr., Austin; Julia Estill, Fredericksburg. Treasurer, Byron Shipp, Austin. Secretary and Editor, J. Frank Dobie, Austin. It was decided to have the 1934 meeting at Austin, April 20–21.

CONTRIBUTORS

J. Mason Brewer under the title of "Juneteenth" contributed an extraordinary collection of slave tales to the 1932 publication of the Texas Folk-Lore Society. Recently a book of verse of his entitled *Negrito* was issued by the Naylor Publishing Company of San Antonio. He is now teaching Spanish in the Booker T. Washington (colored) High School in Dallas. Meantime he is working on a collection of Negro religious folk tales to be called "The Word."

Martha Emmons contributed in 1928 and again in 1932 to the *Publications* of the Texas Folk-Lore Society, the latter contribution affording, through a lovely Negro spiritual she found in Waco, the title for the volume, *Tone the Bell Easy.* A teacher, she is connected with the State Home, at Waco.

David Hall is on the staff of the Fort Worth *Press.* As he for two years specialized in collecting cactus in West Texas and asking, "What is the name of this?" his knowledge of common names for cactus is first-hand.

E. R. Sims is professor of Spanish in the University of Texas. He has been particularly interested in Spanish drama and is collecting Mexican folk-lore.

Mary R. Van Stone, curator of the Art Museum connected with the Archaeological Institute of America, at Santa Fe, New Mexico, has over a period of years been collecting Mexican folk songs and other forms of New Mexican folk-lore.

Hugh McGehee Taylor was born in Montgomery, Alabama, in 1870, and at the age of 19 graduated from the Alabama Polytechnic Institute as a Bachelor of Science in Engineering. Subsequently he received degrees in Civil Engineering from Mexico City. He had been out of college but two years when he went to Mexico and by 1904 was general manager of the Interoceanic Railway. After its consolidation with the Mexican National Railways, he became assistant general manager of that great system and director of construction. In 1913 he resigned to become general manager of the Brazil Railway. With a change of ownership he returned to the United States in 1914 and straightway went to the West Coast of Mexico in connection with the Southern Pacific Railroad. Bryan's orders to American citizens to get out of Mexico, backed by guns in the hands of Carranzistas pointing the way, drove him to Cuba, as chief engineer of the Cuban Northern Railway. During the World War he was in France, first as major and then as lieutenant-colonel, in connection with railway transportation. From 1920 to the present he has lived in Texas, for a while in San Antonio, now in Falfurrias, where, to use his words, he is "running a farm and trying to guess what produce will sell next season." Mr. Taylor speaks Spanish as well as he does English, and he has in his possession a vast fund of folk material connected with Mexico and other Latin-American countries.

INDEX

Every index must draw the line somewhere. The purpose of this one is to afford convenient reference not only to the folk-lore of Texas and the Southwest but to the geography, fauna, flora, and personalities connected with that region. Various names that occur in footnotes and in the text where they carry no power to illuminate, are not indexed.